MOTORCYCLING
A BEGINNER'S MANUAL

Jerry Matthews

Fernhurst Books

British Library Cataloguing in Publication Data
Matthews, Jerry
    Motorcycling: a beginner's manual.
    1. Motorcycling
    I. Title
    796.7

    ISBN 0-906754-53-4

Printed and bound in Great Britain

Published by Fernhurst Books,
33 Grand Parade, Brighton, East Sussex.

Acknowledgements
The author and publishers would like to thank Heron Suzuki Ltd for providing motorcycles and facilities for photography, and Celia White for riding the bikes during the photo sessions.

Photographs
All photographs by John Woodward, except the following:
BMF: page 62
Jerry Matthews: page 9
Superbike/Patrick Gosling: cover
Sir John Whitmore: page 53

Edited and designed by John Woodward
Cover design by Joyce Chester
Typeset by Central Southern Typesetters, Hove
Printed by Ebenezer Baylis, Worcester

CONTENTS

Introduction

When you get your first bike your main concern will be to get over the legal hurdles of training and passing your test. We will give you plenty of help to do that. First of all, we guide you through the complicated legal requirements you must satisfy before you are allowed to ride a motorcycle, scooter or moped on the public roads. We show you how to get through the official Driving Standards Agency (DSA) test. But the main purpose of this book is to help you become a better, more skilful rider. Our aim is to help you get the most fun and enjoyment out of your bike. We give you advice on the choice of bike and riding gear. We explain how a motorcycle works, and how to keep your bike in safe, roadworthy condition. Finally, we offer some information on social activities, touring, motorcycle sport and advanced riding.

We don't intend this book to be a 'teach yourself to ride' manual, however. You can't learn to ride a motorbike out of a book, any more than you can learn to ski, sail, or play tennis out of a book. There is no substitute for practical training, and in fact the law now requires that you complete a basic training course before you can ride on the road. What this book is really trying to do is supplement what you learn on your training course, and give you a ready source of reference and review.

Part one:
Getting to know your bike

Motorcycling means different things to different people. Some ride for the excitement and freedom that they experience. Some like the economy of a motorbike — probably the most efficient form of motorised transport there is. For others, a bike is simply a cheap and fast way to get to work or college, or do the shopping. Whatever attracted your interest at first, you will soon find that owning a motorbike is a lot of fun. It's enjoyable and exciting. It brings you the freedom to go where you want and when you want — across town or across a continent. What's more, it can open up a whole new world of friends and activities.

What makes riding a motorbike so different from driving any other motor vehicle? To start with, motorcyclists themselves are different. They are drawn together by a special camaraderie that non-motorcyclists find hard to understand. Even on the crowded roads of the 1990s they still have time for a friendly wave or flash of headlights to each other. If one's in trouble at the side of the road, it won't be long before another stops to offer help. How many years has it been since that kind of friendship existed in the car-driving world?

Some people think 'bikers' are an undesirable, anti-social lot. But that's more myth than reality. Take the BMF Rally, for example. The BMF (British Motorcyclists Federation) is Europe's largest organisation of road-riding motorcyclists. For the past 30 years it has run the annual BMF Rally, attracting crowds of 20,000 to 30,000 riders, mostly young people. In all those years, the Rally has never witnessed an ugly incident of any kind. Compare that record with an average football crowd or, sad to say, a typical Saturday night down at the pub. The truth is that motorcycling is enjoyed by hundreds of thousands of people in Britain, of all ages, and from all walks of life. There are no social barriers in the world of motorcycling.

The motorbike is different, too. A bike is not just another motor vehicle with two wheels instead of four, and riding a bike is nothing like driving a car. You 'drive' a bike with very small movements of the hands and feet, and very slight – almost subconscious – shifts of body weight. In motion, there is no feeling that you are manhandling a heavy lump of machinery. On the contrary, the bike seems to be an extension of your own body. It's as though you have been given miraculous powers of speed, manoeuvrability and balance. The only other activity I know that produces the physical sensation of motorcycling is skiing. But you need a snow-covered mountain to ski, and you can't very well ski to work unless you happen to be an Alpine herdsman.

Added to the sheer pleasure of riding a motorcycle are its practical advantages over four wheels. It is small, highly manoeuvrable, takes up less space, and can use sections of road that are inaccessible to other vehicles. On a bike, you can get through traffic jams quickly and safely, and once you reach your destination, it's easy to park. Given the traffic conditions in towns and on motorways today, and the unreliability of public transport, there is no better way to get around. It is ecologically friendly as well, since all

● There's no denying that bikes have style, and a mechanical appeal that some find very attractive. To buy such style on four wheels would cost a fortune.

● On the other hand, a motorcycle can also be highly practical. A little step-through bike like this is ideal for nipping round town.

modern bikes use unleaded fuel and, contrary to a popular misconception, the motorcycle engine is no more noisy than other vehicles, provided the silencer is properly maintained. Up to a point, a bike is cheap transportation. But beware. If you get truly bitten by the bug, you will find it's an expensive hobby. A high-powered motorcycle can cost as much to buy as a medium-size car, and cost more to insure and run.

There are obvious disadvantages. You must wear a helmet and protective clothing, and sooner or later you're going to get cold and wet no matter how well you dress. You can't carry nearly as many possessions as you can in a car, and securing even small bundles requires thought and ingenuity. You can only take one passenger at a time – once you're legally entitled to carry a passenger – and you can't carry on much of a conversation with your passenger. Some would see that as a positive advantage. And unhappily, you're much more vulnerable to injury.

Even though the motorcycle accident rate has fallen very sharply in recent decades, the statistics still make grim reading. It doesn't matter how you rationalise the statistics. In any mixture of light and heavy traffic, the lighter vehicle will always be more vulnerable.

◆ A motorbike is the ideal vehicle for negotiating town traffic, able to slip through narrow gaps while car drivers fume at the back of the queue.

We know that most motorcyclists are young men, and young men have a different attitude toward risk-taking, whether riding a bike, driving a car, or piloting a jet plane. Yet despite this, more than half the accidents involving a motorbike and another vehicle are caused by errors of the other driver. Personally, such arguments make little impression on me. What does impress me is the stark fact that car bumpers don't bleed, but motorcyclists do. Therefore, I don't rely on any person or any thing for my safety. I don't assume the other road user will do what I think he should do. I would never count on daytime headlights nor conspicuous clothing to protect me, useful as they may be in certain circumstances. I don't believe that any amount of well-intentioned legislation will make me safer on the road. The only thing that will make me safer is my own skill coupled with the right mental attitude. My every movement and thought when riding is designed to keep control in *my* hands, so I don't have to depend on the actions of anyone else. This is what we mean by defensive riding, and I'll have more to say about this subject later.

Riders of motorcycles, scooters and mopeds must comply with special licensing and training requirements that were brought in with the 1989 Traffic Act. Some of these requirements are very complicated.

Age

If you are 17 or over, you may ride a motorcycle or scooter (or drive a car). If you are 16 you may ride a moped. A moped, simply defined, is a motorcycle weighing less than 250kg, with an engine size of 50cc or less, and restricted mechanically so that it cannot go faster than 30mph. In appearance, there may not be much difference between a motorcycle and moped; most manufacturers style their mopeds to look like powerful machines, but don't be fooled by looks.

Provisional licence

The first thing you must do is apply for a provisional licence. You can get a licence application form at the Post Office, and you have to send the form and the required fee to the Driver and Vehicle Licensing Centre (DVLC) in Swansea. The address and amount of the fee are given on the form. You must not drive or ride on the road until you actually receive the licence, so you should send off for it a fortnight or so before you intend to use it. You may apply for a provisional licence when you are 16, but it won't be valid for a car or motorcycle until your 17th birthday.

Now here's where things start to get complicated. Your provisional licence will entitle you to ride a motorcycle, scooter or moped, and to drive a car and certain other vehicles (provided you have reached the required age). *But the motorcycle, scooter, and moped entitlement will not be 'activated' until you have successfully completed a prescribed course of training with an authorised training body.* You must not ride on the road (except with an authorised instructor as explained below) until you have completed the course and received the appropriate certificate, which will then activate your entitlement. If you buy a new bike, the dealer will deliver it to an authorised training centre. If you buy second-hand, someone (the seller, perhaps, or a relation who has a licence) will have to ride or take it there for you.

Compulsory basic training

The only training schemes that can offer this course, and issue the necessary certificates, are those specifically appointed by the DSA. A motorcycle dealer can tell you which they are, or you can get more information from your local road safety officer or the BMF Rider Training Scheme (see page 63 for address and telephone number). The course itself is straightforward and based on common sense. Everything in it is explained in detail in this book. There are no tests involved, but you have to complete each part satisfactorily before you can move on to the next. The instructor will explain the aims of the course, legal requirements, equipment and clothing. He or she will familiarise you with your bike, show you basic machine checks, and how to start and stop the engine. You will be able to practice simple manoeuvres and braking exercises in a safe place off the road.

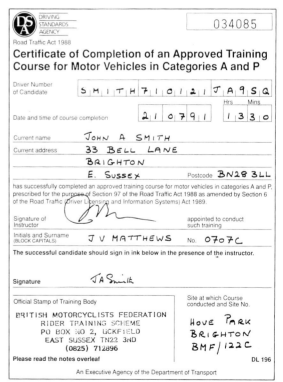

As soon as your instructor thinks you are ready, he or she will take you out on the road. There must not be more than two trainees with each instructor, and you must not ride anywhere on a public road unless you are accompanied by a qualified instructor. The course will last as long as it takes for you to satisfy your instructor that you are competent to ride on the road.

Once you have your certificate (DL 196), take good care of it. Not only does it validate your licence, but you must have it with you when you take the DSA test. The certificate will validate a motorcycle licence even if you did the course on a moped, so if you decide to get a motorcycle after you turn 17 you won't have to retake the course – so long as your certificate is still valid.

Many training centres will have motorcycles or mopeds which you can hire for the course. This means you don't have to worry about getting your own bike to and from the centre, and of course you don't have to buy one until you have completed the course.

The compulsory course is very basic. It doesn't prepare you for the DSA test, and it certainly doesn't give you the skills you need to ride safely and well. Your training centre offers full instruction up to and beyond the test standard. Your instructors are enthusiastic motorcyclists who have a lot to offer; you will probably make friends on the course and have a good time. You would be foolish indeed to quit after basic training even though, legally, you are not obliged to carry on.

Duration of licence

A provisional motorcycle licence is valid for two years. If you do not pass the motorcycle test within the two years before the licence expires, you cannot renew it for a further year. This means you can't ride your bike during that year. There are no exceptions to this rule, so don't leave it too late before applying for the test.

Even more restrictions

You're going to have to tolerate even more legal restrictions during the time between completing the compulsory course and passing the DSA test. The

▲ Compulsory basic training may strike you as dull, but you can learn a lot about your bike and how to get the best out of it. You may even make some new friends!

moral is: get trained and tested and get your full licence as soon as you can. But there's an even better reason for training: on average, the most dangerous time for having an accident is during the first six months of riding. Good training during those early months will go a long way toward making them accident-free.

Until you pass the DSA test:

- You can't ride anything larger than 125cc.
- You have to display L-plates front and rear.
- You can't carry a pillion passenger, even if the passenger holds a full motorcycle licence.
- You're not allowed to ride on the motorway (this restriction applies to learner car drivers as well).

Much of the legislation affecting training, testing and licensing of motorcyclists came into effect in December 1990. Some of the provisions may not apply to you if your licence was issued before then. If you are not sure, you can get more information from the BMF Rider Training Scheme.

LEGAL REQUIREMENTS FOR ALL ROAD USERS

In addition to those laws specific to motorcycles, you are also subject to the laws pertaining to all motor vehicles.

Insurance

You must be insured for any damage you might do to another person or property. This could even be damage sustained when you weren't riding your bike – for example, if it fell over while parked and damaged another vehicle. You must have a Certificate of Insurance issued by the insuring company, and it must specifically cover *you* on the bike you are riding. When you first apply for insurance, the company or agent will probably give you a Cover Note to serve as a temporary Certificate of Insurance, usually valid for 30 days. Make sure you always have either a valid Cover Note or Certificate in your possession. It is illegal to ride without one.

There are three main types of insurance:
- Third Party. This covers your liability for any injury or damage you may cause to another person or property.
- Third Party, Fire and Theft. This covers you as above, and also covers your loss if your own bike is stolen or damaged by fire.
- Comprehensive. This gives you all the cover above, and also covers your loss if your bike is damaged in an accident. Comprehensive cover is normally subject to an 'excess' of £50 or £100, which means the company doesn't pay the first £50 or £100 of each claim. This is a sensible arrangement, since the insurers don't have to handle small claims and can thereby keep premiums down. Also, some companies offer a no-claims discount; if you haven't made any claims for a specified number of years you get a discount on your premium. This can be as high as 40 per cent, so it is to your advantage not to claim for small amounts.

There is another kind of insurance, known as 'Road Traffic Act cover', which gives you only the bare minimum required by law. It's not likely that you could get this cover. In any case, it's generally reserved for drivers who are such a high risk they can't get anything else.

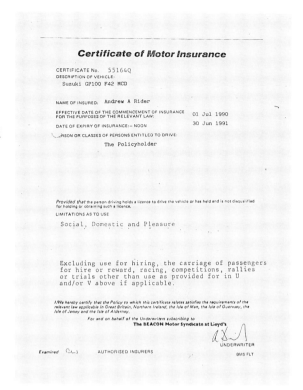

↞ Before you go on the road, make sure you have a valid Certificate of Insurance to cover you on your bike.

Getting insurance if you're young or inexperienced can be an expensive proposition. The smaller the bike the smaller the premium, of course. Oddly enough, a 100cc can be a whole lot cheaper to insure than a 125cc, although there is scarcely any difference between them. Even when you have passed your test and can legally ride any motorcycle, your choice may well be dictated by what you can afford to insure. It pays to shop around, or get a broker to shop around for you. There can be enormous differences between the premiums of one insurer and the next.

Tax

You must pay an annual tax on your bike, known officially as the Vehicle Excise Duty. Here motorcyclists have a big advantage, for the tax on bikes is

◆ **You must have a current tax disc displayed prominently on the bike.**

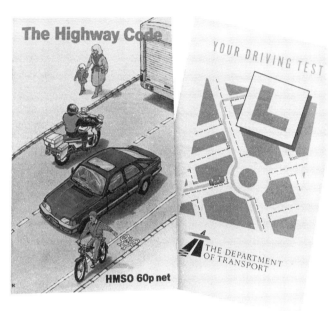

◆ **The Highway Code and 'Your Driving Test' are packed with information. Make sure you read and understand them.**

much cheaper than on cars – even for a superbike it's currently only half as much. You have to display a disc on your bike to show that the tax has been paid, and don't try to get out of it by claiming 'Tax disc in the post'. That's the oldest excuse in the book. There is no reason at all for the disc to be in the post; you can get one in person at most post offices.

MOT test

Three years after the date your bike was first registered it has to be inspected at an authorised garage, and retested again every year thereafter. This is known as the 'MOT test' (after Ministry of Transport, the former name of the Department of Transport). You must have a current Vehicle Test Certificate in your possession if your bike requires one.

Eyesight standard

You must be able to read a car number plate (wearing glasses or contact lenses if you need them) in good daylight at 20.5 metres (about 67 feet). You will be asked to read a number plate when you start your compulsory course, and if you can't meet the standard you won't be able to do the on-road part of it. Your eyesight will also be checked when you take your DSA test.

The Highway Code

Get a copy of the Highway Code, available at almost any bookshop or newsagent. Read it, learn it, and make sure you understand it. Your DSA test examiner will ask you questions about it, and you have to obey it while taking your test.

As the name implies, a motorcycle is a motorised bicycle. The rider of a bicycle makes it go by pedalling with his feet. The power he applies to the pedals is transmitted through a chain to the rear wheel, and this drives the bicycle forward. It will keep going as long as the rider continues pedalling and steering. It will soon fall over when he stops. A motorcycle works the same way, except that a petrol engine does the pedalling. In fact, 100 years ago motorcycles were simply bicycles with small engines bolted on.

The basic principle that worked 100 years ago still applies today: the engine transmits power through gears and a chain or shaft to the bike's rear wheel. But motorcycles have made giant advances since the early days in terms of engine design, frame, suspension, brakes, tyres and electrics. A modern motorbike is a complex piece of machinery, and electronic ignition and other high-tech features are commonplace on all models and sizes. The days when a motorcyclist could achieve almost any repair at the side of the road with a few simple tools are long since gone. But even though few motorcyclists today are fullyfledged mechanics, those who have a basic understanding of what goes on mechanically, and why a motorcycle performs the way it does, are better riders because of it.

Engine

Your bike will have either a two-stroke or a four-stroke engine. Both two- and four-stroke engines have one or more cylinders with a piston moving up and down within each cylinder. A mixture of air and petrol is drawn into the cylinder and exploded by a spark from the spark plug. The explosion forces the piston down, powering the engine; this is called the power stroke. Both kinds of engines also have a carburettor which mixes the air and petrol into a fine mist before it is sucked into the cylinder. The main difference is that the four-stroke engine needs four movements of the piston for every power stroke. Valves operated by cams are timed to open and close during the fourstroke cycle, controlling the flow of the petrol/air mixture in and exhaust gas out. In contrast, a two-stroke engine needs only two movements of the piston for each power stroke. Instead of valves, the piston itself covers and uncovers holes in the cylinder wall (known as ports) as it moves up and down, sucking fuel in and forcing the exhaust out.

The other main difference between these two types of engines is the way they are lubricated. With a four-stroke you put oil into a separate reservoir. The oil is circulated by an oil pump so that it bathes, cools and lubricates all moving engine parts. With a two-stroke, the oil is mixed in with the petrol. On older bikes you actually had to measure out the oil and pour it into the petrol tank. Now, most two-strokes have a separate oil container from which the oil is automatically metered. Two-strokes burn up the oil, so you must continually add it. Four-strokes retain the oil (although there may be a small loss, so you have to top it up from time to time) but you will have to change it by draining out the old and adding new at regular intervals. Whether a two- or four-stroke, oil is the lifeblood of your engine. Neglect it and you will surely ruin your bike.

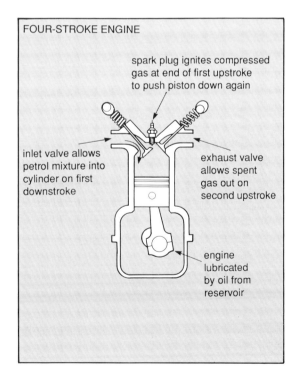

FOUR-STROKE ENGINE

spark plug ignites compressed gas at end of first upstroke to push piston down again

inlet valve allows petrol mixture into cylinder on first downstroke

exhaust valve allows spent gas out on second upstroke

engine lubricated by oil from reservoir

You won't notice much difference between the two kinds of engines when riding. A four-stroke has a bit more engine braking (since there is power on just one stroke out of four) but that won't affect you a whole lot. A two-stroke is a much 'dirtier' engine, however. Because it's burning oil in the cylinder it smokes more and leaves more carbon on the piston and in the exhaust. It's harder to cool, since the oil doesn't circulate. It's not so efficient, and you will get fewer miles per gallon. Nowadays, you will find most two-stroke engines on smaller bikes, mainly 250s or smaller. But they do have certain advantages. Because they don't need a system of valves, cams, cam chains and the like, they are much simpler and more robust than four-strokes.

Your engine cylinders are measured by their cubic capacity (cc) and this determines the size rating of your bike. For example, if it has one cylinder of about 125cc, it's a 125cc motorcycle. If it has four cylinders of around 250cc each, it's a 1000cc.

Throttle and choke

To make the bike go faster you open the throttle. This is done by a simple twist of the wrist on the right-hand bar grip. As a safety precaution the grip will twist back on its own if you let go. All that happens when you twist the grip is that a cable running down from the handlebar opens a valve allowing more of the petrol/air mixture to be drawn into the cylinder. The more drawn in, the faster you go.

To start the engine when it's cold you need a richer petrol/air mixture – more petrol, less air. You get this by operating the choke, a small lever or knob usually found on the handlebar or somewhere under the petrol tank. This chokes off the air supply to the car-burettor. As soon as the engine warms up and is running smoothly, you have to return the choke lever to its normal position or the engine will stall.

◆ **The throttle or 'accelerator' on a bike is a twist-grip on the right-hand handlebar. Ease the grip forward to slow down (left), and twist it back to speed up (right).**

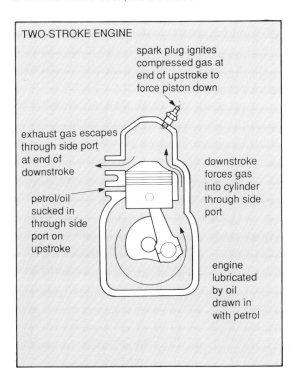

TWO-STROKE ENGINE

spark plug ignites compressed gas at end of upstroke to force piston down

exhaust gas escapes through side port at end of downstroke

petrol/oil sucked in through side port on upstroke

downstroke forces gas into cylinder through side port

engine lubricated by oil drawn in with petrol

Gears and clutch

You need gears to get more power for moving off, accelerating, and going uphill. You need a clutch so you can move off smoothly, change gear, and stop the bike without killing the engine.

To understand how gears work, it's helpful to visualise the gears on a five-speed bicycle. Low gear is when the pedals and chain are driving the large sprocket near the spokes of the back wheel: you get a lot of power for climbing hills, but not much speed. High gear is when the chain is driving the smallest sprocket: you get more speed but less power. This principle also works when you change gears on a motorbike. You need to use low gear when you start off, to get up momentum. As you build up speed you change up to a higher gear. When you have to slow down, or if you see you will need power to accelerate or go up a hill, you change down to a lower gear again. When you stop you put the gears in neutral: this means that the gear wheels are disengaged, allowing the engine to tick over while the bike is standing still.

To change gear, you have to use the clutch. The clutch is a series of friction plates, pressed together by springs, which connect the drive of the engine to the gearbox. You operate the clutch on a motorcycle by pulling in a lever on the left handlebar. This separates the plates and disengages the drive, allowing you to change gear or find neutral. When you ease the clutch lever out again the clutch plates mesh together, taking up the power drive, and off you go.

You change gears by moving a pedal with your left foot. Most bikes now have five or six gears, plus neutral. Pull in on the clutch lever and press down gently on the gear pedal. This takes you from neutral to first (the lowest) gear. To change to a higher gear, pull in on the clutch lever again, and lift the pedal with your left toe back through neutral into second gear. You can then go on up to third, fourth, fifth or even sixth, and back down again.

If you know how to change gear on a car, you will know that you can move the gear lever from, say, first gear to fourth in one movement. You can't do that on a bike. You have to change one gear at a time, up or down, in succession.

◆ The clutch is controlled by a hand lever. With the lever released (top) the clutch is engaged. By squeezing the lever (above) you disengage the clutch, ready to change gear. Make sure you pull on the lever with all four fingers.

◆ You change up through the gears by lifting the gear pedal with your toe as shown. Change down by pressing down on the pedal.

☛ Applying the brakes throws the weight of the bike forward, and this affects the adhesion of the tyres. Here the brakes are off, and the weight is evenly distributed on both wheels. As a result, both the front and back tyre are gripping well.

☛ When the rider slams on the brakes, all the weight is concentrated on the front wheel. See how the front forks have been squeezed down. The weight comes off the back tyre, which has very little grip at this point. Too much back brake pressure could lock the wheel, causing a skid.

Brakes

Your bike will be fitted with two brakes: one on the front wheel and one on the rear. The front brake is operated by a lever on the right handlebar, the rear brake by a pedal under your right foot. It is imperative that you use both the front and rear brakes, and use them correctly.

Front and rear brakes affect the handling of the bike in different ways. Both slow the rotation of their respective wheels, but there the similarity ends. When you brake or slow down on a bike your weight and that of the bike itself shift forward. This means there is a lot more weight pressing down on the front wheel, and as a result the front tyre has a strong grip on the road surface. At the same time, the rear of the machine has become comparatively weightless, so the rear tyre has almost no grip on the road. Why then bother with a rear brake? There is a good reason. If you were to apply only the front brake when riding fast you would slow the front wheel well enough, but the rear wheel would try to keep coming on. It couldn't 'catch up' with the front, of course, so it would tend to step out sideways and this could turn your bike on its side. For a different reason, you would also never use the rear brake by itself when travelling at speed. You would merely succeed in locking up the rear wheel, leaving a long skid mark of burnt rubber, and probably hitting the object you were trying to miss. But there are times, at *slow* speed, when it is better to use the rear brake only.

Correct use of the brakes is the most important thing there is to know about motorcycling. We are going to deal with this vital subject in some detail later on.

Steering

This is one of the most fascinating things about a motorbike, and the way you steer it is what makes riding a bike so much fun. First, think about steering a car. If you want to go right you turn the steering wheel right; in you want to go left you turn the wheel left. Not on a bike! You don't steer a bike by turning the handlebars unless you are going very slowly – almost at a walking speed. You steer by leaning into the direction you want to go.

A motorcycle moving in a straight line has the steering geometry of a cylinder. Imagine you are rolling an unopened tin of beans on its side. The tin will roll along in a straight line. Now imagine that instead of a cylindrical tin you have one shaped like an ice-cream cone, tapering towards one end. This time it will roll in a circle, turning in the direction of the smaller end.

The more sharply it's tapered, the tighter it will turn. When you lean on a bike, you change its steering geometry from a cylinder to a cone, and it immediately starts to turn. The more you lean, the more you are 'tapering the cone' and the tighter the turning circle. You can get the same effect as leaning by exerting very gentle pressure on the handlebars opposite to the direction you want to turn.

As you turn, certain natural forces take over. Think about the car again. As the car turns it is pulled in an outward direction by what is known as centrifugal force. This force is working against the car and if the driver is taking it too fast he may have a struggle holding the road. But on a bike, the forces are working in your favour. As you lean into the bend, gravity pulls you and your bike downward, but centrifugal force pulls you outward. All you have to do to maintain just the right equilibrium is gently adjust your angle of lean and the amount of pressure on the handlebars. It sounds complicated in print, but in practice it comes as naturally as breathing. The first time you experience a sweeping bend on a clear road you will understand what I am talking about.

One critical factor in the equation, however, is tyre grip on the road. If you lose grip, either because you hit a slippery patch on the road or because your tyres are worn, you are going to be in trouble. This is why tyre and road-surface conditions are so vitally important to motorcyclists.

The description given here of gears, brakes, clutch and throttle controls applies to the vast majority of motorcycles sold in Britain today. There are a few exceptions, mainly on the small, step-through machines, but your training scheme instructor will show you how all the controls work on your bike.

◢ **When you lean into a bend, gravity pulls you down while centrifugal force pulls you outward. As long as your tyres are gripping the road well, you will sweep round without consciously turning the handlebars. It feels good!**

Even if you are a learner and restricted to a 125cc motorcycle you have a wide range to choose from. At the last count, there were nearly 40 models of learner motorcycles on the market in the UK. These are mainly of three kinds.

First is the step-through, or scooter-type bike. These you tend to sit in rather than sit on. They admittedly have a rather staid image, but they are easy to ride and inexpensive to run. If your main concern is cheap and reliable transport, one of these could be the bike for you. It would also suit a small person, who might have trouble with a tall-in-the-saddle machine.

If you are long-legged, you may prefer the second option, a trail bike. These are so-called because they are designed for riding both on the road and in the rough, although only a small number ever get off the tarmac. Most are ridden in town, where their narrow width and agile handling make them well suited to dense traffic. They have a reassuring 'big-bike' feel about them and are pleasant to ride. The knobbly tyres grip well in rough conditions, but they have marginally less grip than normal motorcycle tyres on wet roads.

The third option is the standard road bike. This can be a fairly bland commuter bike or something that looks as though it just came off the race track. Appearances notwithstanding, there isn't much difference in the speed or performance of any learner 125, so choose the one that fits you best.

If you're 16 and restricted to a moped you still have more than 30 models to choose from, with the same variety of choice as the learner motorcycles described above. But no matter what style of moped you decide on, you'll never be able to wring more than about 30mph out of it. (There are ways to improve the performance of a moped by mechanical modification, but then it ceases to be a moped and would be illegal for a 16-year-old to ride. Before you attempt any such modification on your bike, think how it might affect insurance costs and resale value.)

When you pass your test and can legally ride any motorcycle your only limitation will be the state of your bank balance. You now have a dazzling choice of something like 160 different models. There isn't room to describe and discuss them here. Talk to your training scheme instructors. In all likelihood they will have an impressive range of bikes and will be only too happy to talk about them.

Many motorcyclists will insist that they choose their bike for performance, reliability, economy or other virtuous reasons. But the truth is that most of us see a motorcycle as a reflection of our own personality. We therefore buy the one that projects the kind of image we want to project. Marketing men are well aware of this, which is why they give us such a wide choice. How do you account for the following of a bike like the Harley-Davidson? It's very expensive. No one says it's especially fast, nor that it handles particularly well. It is most certainly not economical to run. But it makes its owner feel different and feel good. That's part of what motorcycling is all about.

◄ **Motorbikes come in all shapes and sizes. You will have to start with something modest, but once you pass your test, you can buy and ride anything you can afford.**

You've got your bike. It's taxed and insured. You've got your licence, and you're ready to go. Now all your need are helmet, gloves, boots, leathers and waterproofs! Well, I did warn you motorcycling could be a costly pastime. But the right gear is essential protection both from weather and from injury.

Helmet

The law says you must wear a helmet, and even if there were no such law you would be stupid not to wear one. All helmets sold in Britain must comply with the exacting standards set by the British Standards Institution (BSI). Currently, helmets have to meet BSI Standard BS6658, and every helmet on sale must have a BSI sticker with a kitemark to certify that it does comply. When you buy your helmet, be sure to look for the BSI kitemark.

You have a wide choice of helmets. The most popular kind today is the full-face or integral helmet with a hinged visor. This helmet gives maximum protection for your head and face. But the open-face helmet is also popular with many riders, possibly because it's lighter in weight and offers better vision. Whatever you choose, the two important considerations are that it meets the standard, and that it fits your head without causing discomfort or distraction. If you have never worn a helmet before, you'll find it a bit oppressive at first. But you'll soon get used to it provided it's a good fit. When you try on a helmet be sure to secure the strap. The helmet should fit snugly but not so tightly as to hurt your head. Make sure you cannot move your head around inside it, and you must not be able to pull it off with the strap still fastened.

Helmets are made of various kinds of plastic materials and glass fibre, but all materials must meet the BSI standard. Some plastics react to paint and adhesives, so don't paint your helmet or plaster stickers all over it. Never buy a second-hand helmet. It may have sustained damage which you can't see and won't know about until you put it to the test. By then, it's too late. Make sure the strap is well-secured when riding. The helmet won't do you much good if it flies off your head. Finally, buy the best helmet you can afford. After all, it's your head.

Eye protection

You will want to use some kind of visor or goggles to protect your eyes from rain, insects, dust, and other flying objects. The flip-up visor is the most practical and popular kind. All must comply with BSI standards, which currently are BS4110/ZA, BS4110/XA, or BS4110/YA. Make sure your visor or goggles are stamped with one of these standards; otherwise it is illegal to use them.

One problem with any form of eye protection is misting up, especially in cold or wet weather or at night. You can spend money on various kinds of anti-mist sprays and lotions, but the best and by far the cheapest remedy is a drop of washing-up liquid. Rub it on both sides and polish it off with a clean paper tissue. Scratches are another problem. All visors and goggles sold now must be coated with a scratch-resistant substance, but sooner or later they will scratch and must be replaced. A scratched visor is a serious hazard, especially at night.

Gloves and boots

Next to your head, your hands and feet are your most vulnerable parts. Always wear gloves when riding, even in warm weather. Wear leather gloves, not plastic or fabric ones. I have two pairs – unlined for summer and fur-lined for winter – plus waterproof overmitts for wet-weather wear.

A good pair of boots or sturdy shoes is essential for protecting your feet and ankles from injury and also from the cold and wet. Few things can drain your alertness and concentration as fast as cold, soggy feet. Boots are best, but what you need will depend on what and where you ride. If you use a little step-through bike for the local shopping or short commutes you are unlikely to need or want a rugged pair of motorbike boots. But avoid plimsolls, high heels, sandals and other kinds of flimsy shoes and dangling laces which could get tangled up in the controls.

Leather clothing

Leather is the traditional material for motorcyclists, and despite all the advances in new fibres and fabrics, it is still the best. It's not just because of its macho image, and it doesn't have to be black; you can get a leather jacket or suit to match your bike or whatever you like. Leather provides excellent wind and weather resistance, but its main benefit has to do with protecting yourself from injury. Perhaps the most common accident involves being knocked off your bike and sliding down the hard road surface. The friction generated by a high-speed slide will melt nylon, shred other fabrics and leave your bare skin exposed to unthinkable injury. Leather can take it, and unless you have the misfortune to hit something your chances

☛ **A one-piece waterproof suit will keep the rain and spray out, but it's best to wear leather underneath.**

of coming out with just a few bruises are reasonably good. When you buy leather, though, make sure it was made for motorcycling. There are a lot of motorbike-style jackets sold in clothing shops, but their materials and stitching may not have what it takes.

Waterproofs

Leather is fine in a brief shower, especially if you treat it with a leather dressing from time to time, but in prolonged rain it will soon become a soggy mess. You will want some kind of waterproof clothing as well. There is plenty to choose from, and you can get almost any kind of waterproof suit you need. In summer, I like an unlined, one-piece oversuit that can be slipped on over leathers or other clothing. In winter a heavily-lined two-piece suit offers good protection, but I still prefer something that can go on over leathers. Bear in mind that whatever you wear must fit you in the riding position, not just standing around, and you will want to be able to wear warm clothing underneath. The collar must fit securely and comfortably, cuffs should be close-fitting so gloves can go over them, and leg fastenings should be snug and secure without loose and flapping ends. The first time you find yourself standing in the rain in bare feet, putting on your weatherproofs, you will wish you had found a suit that will slip on over boots.

Conspicuous clothing

This is a favourite hobby-horse of the road safety lobby, and there are those who would oblige us by law to equip our bike and person with all kinds of reflective and conspicuous accessories. My own advice is to use a little common sense. A motorbike is smaller than other road vehicles and less easily seen. It is in your interest to make sure that you are seen. In certain weather and visibility conditions, switching on your headlight, wearing a reflective Sam Brown belt or a brightly-coloured tabard may help. But this kind of gadgetry is of less value than your own riding attitude and style. If you want other motorists to see you – and react to having seen you – your best course is to ride in a positive and assured manner, be in control of your bike and your patch of road, and be in the right position on the road at all times.

HANDLING THE BIKE

When you get your bike, the first thing you need to do is get the feel of handling it and pushing it around. A motorcycle or moped is a lot heavier than a bicycle, and if you let it fall over you could cause some expensive damage. It's far easier to control a motorbike when you are sitting on it, but since there are many times when you will have to move it around when you're off it – putting it on or off the stand, or pushing it into a parking space – you need to master that first.

Always stand on the left side of the bike. This gives you access to the side and centre stands and a better angle for controlling the front brake with your right hand so the bike doesn't roll away from you. Keep the weight of the bike slightly towards you: if it starts to fall when it's leaning your way, you can easily hold it up, but if it starts to fall away from you, especially if it's a heavier machine, you may not be able to hold it. Push the bike forwards, backwards, around in a circle and up and down an incline. Make sure you're always able to reach the front brake lever.

Next, practise putting it on the centre stand. Most bikes have two stands: a side stand which props the bike up in leaning position, and a centre stand which is more stable and holds the bike upright and level. Trail bikes and some others have only the side stand. Putting a bike on its centre stand, even if it's a heavy motorcycle, is easy to do once you get the knack, and it doesn't need a lot of strength. Stand facing the bike on its left-hand side, with your left hand gripping the left handlebar and your right hand holding the bike somewhere underneath the seat (some models have a convenient grab rail there). Push the centre stand down with your right foot so that both legs of the stand are firmly on the ground. Now, press down hard on the stand with your foot, and at the same time lift up with your right hand. Use your left hand merely to steady the handlebars. The bike should go up onto the stand with little effort.

To take it off, stand facing the bike as before with your hands in the same place and push forward, making sure that when it starts to roll the weight comes toward you. As the stand starts to come up, arrest it with your foot to stop it bashing the underside of the bike, and be ready to grab the front brake lever if the machine starts to roll away. Pushing the bike off the centre stand while sitting on it is not recommended.

You're now ready to get on. Hold the front brake lever with your right hand so the machine doesn't roll out from under you. Throw you leg over and sit in the saddle, with both hands on the bars. Your left foot should now be on the ground, and your right foot holding the rear brake. You should be sitting comfortably, leaning forward a bit, with all controls to hand. You should get the feeling very quickly that the bike 'fits' you – that it is an extension of yourself.

◆ To put the bike on its stand, first push the stand down with your foot, and hold it there.

◆ Holding the bike by the left handlebar and under the seat, lift it up and back with your right hand.

◆ If it is well balanced, the bike should go up on its stand with little effort.

The first thing you need to operate is the petrol tap. Petrol is gravity-fed from the tank to the carburettor, and most bikes have an on/off tap located somewhere under the tank. This should be switched off when the bike is parked. You can switch it on before you get on the bike, but you must be able to operate it while riding. This is because most taps also have a reserve position which gives you another two litres or so of petrol when the main feed runs dry. You don't want to be fumbling around trying to find the tap if you run out in traffic. Know how to reach it and operate it without looking down.

You will probably find the ignition lock in an obvious place somewhere near the centre of the handlebars, although a few manufacturers still tuck it away in awkward places. The ignition lock has two main positions: on and off. The one on your bike may have other positions – to operate a steering lock perhaps, or let you leave lights on when the bike is parked. Your instructor will show you what they are. When the ignition is off everything on the bike, including lights and horn, is dead. When you turn the key to switch on, the instrument panel will light up. A green light will tell you that the gears are in neutral, and there will also be red warning lights for oil pressure or generator. The red lights should go off as soon as you start the engine; if not, stop it again and find out why.

Somewhere on the right or left handlebar (positions vary on different machines) you will find the horn button, switches to operate the headlights (on/off and high/low) and a switch for the turn indicator lights. The indicators don't cut off automatically on most motorbikes, like they do on cars; be sure to switch them off manually when you're riding on the road, or other road users will misinterpret your intentions and you could be in danger.

You will also find the 'kill switch' on one handlebar. This cuts out the ignition. It is for emergency use only, so don't use it for switching off routinely. Unfortunately, it's rather easy to switch off accidentally, and idle fingers may tamper with it when you leave the motorcycle parked. So if you can't get your bike started, or if it cuts out on you while riding along, check the kill switch!

◆ You'll probably find the petrol tap under the tank. Switch it off when you leave the bike.

◆ Most of the controls are on the handlebars. On this bike, the light switches, indicators and horn are on the left . . .

◆ . . . while the 'kill switch' is on the right.

As mentioned earlier, you control the front brake and throttle with your right hand and the clutch with your left hand; you change gears with your left foot, and operate the rear brake with your right foot. We explained how the choke works in an earlier section. You will find the control for operating it either near the handlebars or under the tank. It only remains to describe the starting mechanism.

If your bike has electric start, you simply push a button. Most smaller machines have a kickstart lever just behind the right footrest, but this is also easy to use. You may have seen films of motorcyclists starting up in the old days by lifting themselves up in the saddle and then coming down on the kickstart with all their weight – but if you do that on a small modern machine you're more likely to break off the kickstart. All you have to do is prod the lever gently with your foot until you feel resistance. Then give a short, sharp downward kick. Once you get the hang of it, the bike will normally start on the first kick every time.

▸ **You may find it easier to raise yourself up to use the kickstart, but don't come down on the lever with all your weight. There's no need, and you might break it.**

☛ **To get moving, first pull in the clutch lever.**

☛ **Press down with your left foot to engage first gear.**

☛ **Gently let out the clutch lever until the engine note changes.**

So now you're ready to start up the engine. You're sitting comfortably with both hands on the handlebars, right foot holding the rear brake, left foot on the ground. Make sure the petrol tap is on. If the engine is cold, use the choke. Turn the ignition key and the green neutral light should come on. But just to make sure you're in neutral, rock the bike forward a bit. You will feel resistance if it's in gear. When you're happy that everything is in order, push the starter button if you have one. If you have a kickstart, let go of the rear brake and hold the front one instead. Now use the kickstart as we explained in the previous paragraph. The amount of throttle you need to use when starting up varies from engine to engine; as a general rule, don't use much throttle if you're using the choke. You certainly don't need to rev the engine excessively the way some learners like to do.

Return the choke lever to its normal position as soon as the engine is running smoothly. Now you can start to master control of the throttle and clutch, enabling you to move forward under power. This can be a bit tricky at first, but your instructor will give you all the help you need. Put the bike in first gear by pulling in on the clutch lever and pushing down on the gear-change pedal. You will hear a definite 'clunk' as the gear engages, and the green neutral light will go out. Don't let go of the clutch lever yet. Open the throttle by twisting the grip slowly until the engine starts to speed up, but don't rev it hard. Now, ease out on the clutch lever *very gently* until you feel the clutch start to bite – that is when you can feel the bike try to edge forward and the engine starts to strain. Hold the clutch at biting point and open the throttle a bit more, letting the bike move slowly forward. Keep opening the throttle gently and easing out the clutch lever as the bike picks up momentum until it is moving forward smoothly. Don't worry if you stall the engine a few times, or have difficulty at first getting the co-ordination just right. Your instructor will give you plenty of time to get it right.

Ready to ride away? Not quite. Before we let you go, there are two more things you need to know. One is the system of motorcycle control, which is mainly about looking behind and letting other road users know what you are going to do. The other is how to use the brakes correctly.

◆ **Twist the right-hand grip to give the engine more throttle.**

◆ **Gently release the clutch lever as you increase the throttle, and off you go!**

THE SYSTEM OF MOTORCYCLE CONTROL

The system of motorcycle control is an exercise or drill which you must follow *in sequence* before making any manoeuvre or approaching any hazard such as a bend in the road, another vehicle, or a change of road surface. In its simplest form, the system consists of rear observation and signalling. Added to it, when on the road, are positioning, speed, gear changes and use of the horn. The system is the basis for every manoeuvre you will do on a motorbike: moving off, turning right or left, slowing down, stopping. Using the system correctly will give you time to react to any change in traffic before you commit yourself to the manoeuvre.

The basic system is as follows:

1 LOOK BEHIND
2 SIGNAL
3 LIFESAVER
4 MANOEUVRE

Let's take them in turn.

Look behind

Never move off, change direction or slow down without knowing what's behind you. It seems obvious, doesn't it? But after years of riding I am still amazed at the number of motorcyclists I see (usually small bikes with L-plates) zooming all over the road in happy disregard of what might be coming up behind them. Look first. All bikes are now fitted with mirrors and you should use them. But you also need to *turn your head* and look behind – over your right shoulder if you're moving off or turning right, and over your left shoulder if turning left.

Signal

You've looked behind and it's safe to manoeuvre. Now let others know what you intend to do. Give an appropriate signal. When you're first learning you should use arm signals as well as indicator lights. Sometimes the lights on a smaller bike don't show up well in daylight. Also you must learn to steer the bike

LOOK BEHIND

SIGNAL

singlehandedly without wobbling. But for normal on-road riding you wouldn't use arm signals unless there were good reason to do so – bulb failure, making two turns in quick succession, doing something unexpected (turning into a private drive when there is a major crossroad just beyond it) or if you want to emphasise your intentions.

When you use arm signals they should be exactly as shown in the Highway Code – arm straight out from your shoulder, palm extended, fingers together. Hold the signal for a quick count to three, then get both hands back on the bars.

Lifesaver

You've looked. You've signalled. Now take one more quick look over your shoulder before you go. This is called the lifesaver, and for good reason. No matter how well the mirrors are fitted or adjusted, there is a blind spot immediately behind every motorcycle. In the short interval between your first look behind and

actually changing course, a fast-moving vehicle may have come into that blind spot, with disastrous consequences if you change direction into its course. Give the lifesaver just before you move, but not so late that you can't change your mind if necessary. I sometimes dramatise the blind spot and need for a lifesaver by asking a learner to sit on his bike in the riding position, using the mirrors to check behind. It is very easy to walk up and touch him on the shoulder without coming into the mirrors' range of vision at any time.

Manoeuvre

You've looked, signalled, and given the lifesaver. Now GO! Move decisively and swiftly, without hanging about. Your movement must be a definite one, not a gradual drift across the road.

The whole system should be in sequence, with four separate and distinct movements. Eventually, it should become automatic.

LIFESAVER

GO!

As we mentioned earlier, learning how to use the brakes correctly is probably the most important thing there is to know about motorcycling. Many accidents would never occur if more motorcyclists knew how to brake properly. Let's look at a few examples:

- You're riding happily down the road, observing the speed limit. Suddenly, a car pulls out in front of you from a side road – the driver either didn't see you or else he misjudged your speed. You do what a lot of riders would do – you panic, grab the front brake lever with all your strength, and stamp down on the rear brake pedal as hard as you can. Inevitably your wheels lock up, you go into a skid and crash. To add insult to injury, the other driver continues on his way, unaware of what has happened to you.

- Friday night rush hour. It's raining and you want to get home. The traffic light ahead is showing green and you think you can get across. Then it turns to amber. The vehicle ahead slows to stop and you have to pull up sharply. You apply firm pressure on front and rear brakes, but your front tyre loses grip on the wet road surface and you crash into the back of the car in front of you.

- You're enjoying a pleasant run on a winding country road. Suddenly you find yourself in a sharp bend to the right. You have misjudged it, you're going too fast, and you're not going to make it. You apply front and rear brakes firmly in an effort to slow down. Before you know what's happened you are sitting in the ditch, and your motorbike is a pile of bent metal several yards down the road.

These three examples are the three most common accident situations for motorcyclists. In each example, there could have been a different outcome if the rider had braked correctly.

Earlier, we explained how the front and rear brakes cause the machine to react in different ways because of changing weight distribution when they are applied. The front brake is much the more powerful of the two. The other thing to understand is that the brakes do not stop the motorcycle, they only slow the wheel rotation. The grip of the tyres on the road surface stops the bike. Excessive braking, as in the first example above, will lock the wheels so that the tyres

lose grip and the bike goes into a skid. A skilful rider, feeling the rear wheel lock up, can ease off the brake and probably keep control of the bike. But once the front wheel locks there is little hope for staying upright.

There are some basic rules for braking which you must not only know in theory, but must also be able to use in practice:

- On a *dry road* with a *good surface*, most of your braking force should be on the front brake. Some instructors talk about 75 per cent front, 25 per cent rear. I am not quite sure how you measure braking pressure in percentage terms, but the point is you apply considerably more pressure on the front than on the rear.

➤ On a dry road the front brake is the most effective, so put more pressure on the front brake than on the rear.

- A *wet road* gives you a lot less grip, so you ease off the front brake to prevent the front wheel locking and skidding. Some say 50 per cent front, 50 per cent rear. The main thing to remember is that front brake pressure must be far lighter in wet and slippery conditions.
- If you find yourself on a really *treacherous road surface* such as snow, mud, loose chippings, oil or wet leaves, avoid braking as much as you can. If you have to slow down, keep it to a gentle prod on the rear brake. Leave the front alone.
- At *very slow speed*, for example if you are riding at walking pace through dense traffic, use the rear brake only. The more powerful front brake can throw you off balance at slow speed.

Never brake while you are cornering. It will throw the bike off balance, and could throw you in the ditch.

- Brake only when you are *moving upright and in a straight line*. If you brake when you are leaning over, you will instantly destroy that equilibrium we talked about in the section on steering, and the bike will fall over. You can prove this to yourself with a simple little exercise. Walk alongside your bike pushing it in a straight line and keeping it upright. Apply the front brake. The bike will dive forward when you brake, but you can easily hold it upright. Now do the same thing while pushing the bike in a circle. But be very careful this time, for when you hit the brake the bike will try to fall into the circle. Take care not to drop it.

Coming back to the three accidents described earlier, the first was clearly a case of excessive braking causing wheel lock up. This is a difficult one because the most experienced rider can have a moment of panic and over-react. There may be occasions when you simply do not have time to react differently. But correct and controlled braking will often enable you to stay upright and stop in time. In the near future, more motorcycles are likely to be fitted with anti-lock braking systems. In my view, these will be well worth the cost.

The second example showed the consequences of applying too much front brake on a wet road. In the third example the rider got into trouble when he was well into the bend, too late to brake. What can you do if you get yourself into this kind of situation? One possibility is to use the width of the road to get upright again and then brake hard. If there is no other option, you might be able to save it by using the rear brake only. But the moment you hit the front brake in a fast bend, you've lost it.

In all three situations, of course, the rider might have avoided getting into trouble in the first place. He might have anticipated that another road user would do the unexpected; he might have expected the light to change and slowed in time; he might have done a better job of planning the bend, adjusting his speed and dropping down to a lower gear before it was too late. But again we are drifting into the subject of defensive riding, which I shall come back to later.

You're now ready to move off, applying what you have learned about clutch and throttle control and what you know about the system of motorcycle control.

You are ready to go at the side of the road. Your bike is in gear. You are holding the rear brake with your right foot, left foot on the ground.

1 LOOK BEHIND. If all is clear,
2 SIGNAL your intention to move out.
  If you used an arm signal, place both hands back on the bars. Now
3 LIFESAVER. If it is still clear,
4 MOVE OFF smoothly and smartly.

LOOK BEHIND   **SIGNAL**   **LIFESAVER**   **GO!**

DO make sure your bike is in gear before you start looking and signalling. DO make sure you really look behind, DON'T just bob your head to satisfy your instructor. DO look at the road ahead, DON'T look down at the controls. DO lift your feet smartly onto the footrests, DON'T paddle off with them pushing and dragging. DO cancel your indicators once you are underway.

Part two: On the road

It is easy to describe a good motorcyclist: one who is in the right position at all times, in the right gear and travelling at the right speed, aware of the movements of other traffic and always thinking ahead about possible changes in traffic and road conditions. It is easy to describe this paragon of riding skills, but not so easy to become one yourself without a lot of work. The place to start is the system of motorcycle control, described in the last section. Putting the system into practice will enable you to achieve many of the objectives of good motorcycling. It may seem awkward and a bit artificial at first, but when it starts to come smoothly and effortlessly you will be well on the way to becoming a skilful rider.

The best place to start applying the system is on a right turn. This is a complex manoeuvre, and potentially a dangerous one, because you are at risk from traffic coming from several directions. You will be turning across the right-of-way of oncoming traffic. There is also a danger that traffic behind you may try to overtake just as you swing out. Vehicles may pull out from the left or right, and there is the further risk of pedestrians crossing in front of you. For these reasons, the manoeuvre must be executed with care and precision. Your training scheme instructors will spend a lot of time on quiet roads with you, helping you to perfect it.

The manoeuvre is separated into two parts. The first part gets you into the centre of the road ready for the turn; the second part takes you through the turn itself. Let's go through it step by step. You are riding in a position on the left-hand side of the road, and you plan to turn right into a side road a short distance ahead. You would not normally make a right turn from the left-hand side except on a very narrow road, so your first objective is to get to the centre of the road:

1 Look behind. If there is another vehicle moving up fast behind you, hold it for a moment until clear, then look behind again.
2 Signal your intention to move right.
3 Adjust your speed, and consider changing to a lower gear.
4 Give a Lifesaver.
5 Move smartly over to a position just left of the centre of the road. Make your move a decisive one, not a gradual drift across.

You are now on course for the turn:

1 Look behind.
2 Signal. (You can leave your indicator lights going throughout the manoeuvre.)
3 Adjust your speed and change gear.
4 If necessary, sound your horn to make sure other drivers or pedestrians see you. (You use the horn to say 'I am here', not to say 'Get out of my way'.)
5 At this point it may be necessary to give way, either to oncoming traffic or to a pedestrian crossing the road.

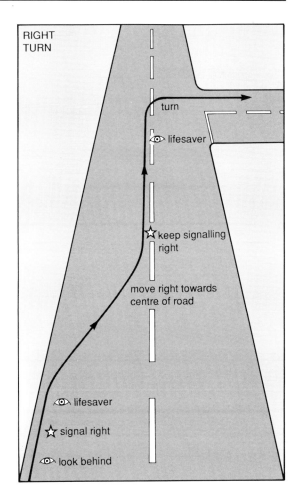

6 The moment the road is clear, give a lifesaver, then GO. Don't dither and don't take time for another arm signal. You are like a sitting duck in a very vulnerable spot on the road. Move out of it quickly, making the turn without swinging out to the left and without cutting the corner.
7 Once you have completed the turn, accelerate out at a safe speed. Be sure to cancel your indicators.

1 Look behind . . .

2 Signal . . .

3 Lifesaver . . .

4 Move to centre . . .

5 Look behind . . .

6 Signal . . .

7 Adjust speed, lifesaver . . .

8 And turn.

There are several errors riders make when executing a right turn. Work at it and try to avoid them. The most common faults are:

- Failing to change down to a lower gear. If you stay in too high a gear you will not have the power to accelerate or to get out of trouble if the situation gets tricky.
- Signalling too soon. (Is he turning into the petrol station just ahead or the side road further along?)
- Signalling too late, causing the vehicle behind to brake or swerve.
- Failing to hold a steady course, especially by swinging left before turning right. Remember that other vehicles may be overtaking on your left as you go right. Don't swing out into their path.
- Braking, changing gear or accelerating during the turn. The basic rule is brake, adjust speed and change gear *before* the turn; hold a constant speed *during* the turn; and accelerate *out of* the turn.

LEFT TURNS

The left turn is not as difficult nor as dangerous as the right turn, but it still needs to be done correctly and precisely. One danger is that as you slow to make the turn, another vehicle – even a bicycle – may come up from behind you on your left side. Don't assume that your inside is clear without looking first, and be sure to give good indication of your intended movements. You would normally be on course on the left-hand side of the road, and the system is applied as follows:

1 Look behind, over your right shoulder.
2 Signal your intention to turn left.
3 Slow down and gear down.
4 Look behind again, over your right shoulder.
5 Signal. Consider sounding your horn if necessary.
6 Give a lifesaver, over your *left* shoulder.
7 Complete the turn without swinging right. Make sure you don't end up on the wrong side of the road.

The commonest left-turn fault is failing to slow down and gear down in good time, forcing you to brake when you are in the turn.

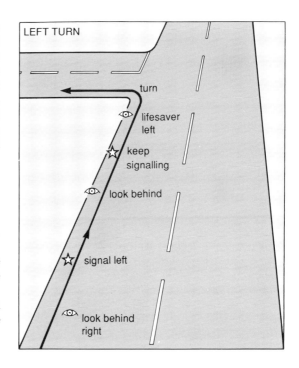

LEFT TURN

turn

lifesaver left

keep signalling

look behind

signal left

look behind right

1 Look behind . . .   2 Signal . . .   3 Adjust speed . . .   4 Lifesaver!   5 And turn.

The main thing you must think about as you approach any crossroad – whether it's your right-of-way or a give-way junction – is how much you can see down the road to the left and right. You may have a clear view, or it may be blocked by parked cars, trees or other obstructions. If you can, position yourself somewhat more to the right to give yourself a better view down the road to the left, and to give any traffic coming out from that road a better view of you. Adjust your speed and gear according to how much you can see. If you have a good view and you can see the way is clear, drop down a gear to give yourself more power if needed, and keep going.

If it is a give-way junction be prepared to stop, but don't stop unnecessarily when you can see the way is clear. The driver in a vehicle behind will expect you to keep going, and may not be able to stop in time. If you come to a 'Stop' sign, bear in mind that the sign is there for good reason – probably because it's a dangerous junction with poor visibility. You *must* stop, which means a complete halt with foot down, and be sure to stop at the white line. Look right, left, then right again followed by a lifesaver before proceeding.

Traffic lights

Traffic lights follow a definite sequence. If you know what that sequence is, you are better able to plan your approach to a junction controlled by lights. Traffic lights also have a precise meaning which you must know. Let's review them in sequence.

RED means 'Stop'. OK, we all agree on that. Red is followed by

RED AND AMBER, which also means 'Stop'. It does *not* mean 'Get ready to go'. You can put your bike in gear and get ready to move, but you must not start to move until green is showing.

GREEN means 'Go *if the way is clear*'. It does not mean 'Go regardless'. Don't move off on green without looking to be sure the way *is* clear. If you hit or are hit by something in the junction it will do no good to argue you had the green light. After green comes

AMBER, which means 'Stop'. Contrary to popular belief, it does not mean 'Hurry up before the light turns red'. There are two situations when you can continue on amber, however. One is if you have

already crossed the stop line *before* the light changes from green to amber (but don't kid yourself by crossing *after* it has changed). The other is if your pulling up might cause an accident – for example, if another vehicle is bearing down so closely from behind that it might hit you if you brake.

It is important, therefore, to apply the system at traffic lights just as you would when approaching any other hazards. Look behind to assess the situation there. Adjust your speed, and drop down a gear to give you a reserve of power and acceleration. Be ready to use your horn if necessary – if a pedestrian looks set to dash across, for example. Plan your approach speed so you can stop if the light changes without being hit from behind. Never speed up, in the hope of getting through, because that will make it more difficult to stop if you must.

You would normally change to neutral while waiting at a traffic light. But if you are in heavy traffic and you believe the light is about to change, it's better to wait momentarily in gear so you can move off without delay once green shows and it is safe to proceed. Don't forget the lifesaver before you move.

◄ If you're stuck at a red light, put the bike in neutral and cover the rear brake.

A roundabout is a crossroad with an island in the middle. Road designers position roundabouts where two or more busy roads come together in order to keep traffic flowing smoothly and quickly. As you approach a roundabout, think of it as a crossroad, and apply the system on your approach as you would a normal left turn, right turn, or as if you were going straight across. Let's take them one by one, starting with the easiest manoeuvre.

Turning left

Your approach is the same as for the left turn described in the preceding section. Holding your course on the left-hand side of the road you:

1 Look behind, over your right shoulder.
2 Signal that you will turn left off the roundabout. You should use indicators in preference to arm signals on roundabouts, and keep the indicators going until you complete the manoeuvre.
3 Slow down and change gear.
4 Give way to any traffic on the roundabout, *but keep going if the way is clear.*

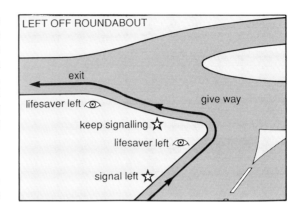

5 Give a lifesaver to the left just as you enter the roundabout, to be sure nothing has come up on your left side.
6 Keep to the left until your exit. Keep your left indicator going. Give a lifesaver to the left just before you exit.
7 Adjust your speed, gears and course when you leave the roundabout.

1 Look behind . . .

2 Signal, using indicator . . .

3 Adjust speed and gear . . .

4 Prepare to give way . . .

5 Lifesaver left as you enter . . .

6 Keep the indicator going for the turn.

Going straight across

Again, you treat the approach as you would a normal crossroad which you were going straight across.

1 Normally, you would approach in the left-hand lane (or on the left of a single-lane approach road), but if that lane is blocked by traffic you may use the right-hand lane.

2 Do not give any signals on your approach.

3 Give way to traffic on the roundabout, but keep going if the way is clear.

4 Give a lifesaver to the left just as you enter the roundabout.

5 Keep to the left, but watch for traffic entering from the next approach road.

6 As soon as you pass the exit before the one you intend to take, look left, signal left, then give a final lifesaver left just before you leave the roundabout.

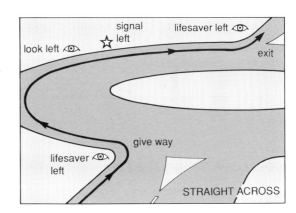

If your approach was from the right-hand lane, you will need to vary your position on the roundabout somewhat. Instead of keeping left, you should go straight across and take up a position near the centre island so that you can follow the curve of the island round. Then, as soon as you have cleared the exit before the one you intend to take, apply the system for manoeuvring back to the left. There is good reason for this. You should always avoid getting stuck between two lanes of traffic on roundabouts. Either position yourself near the centre island so nothing can squeeze you out on your right side, or near the outer rim so nothing can squeeze you from the left.

1 **Don't signal on the approach . . .**

2 **Approach in the left-hand lane . . .**

3 **Prepare to give way . . .**

4 **Enter and position yourself on the left . . .**

5 **Near your exit, signal left . . .**

6 **Lifesaver left as you exit.**

Turning right

It may be helpful to consider this manoeuvre in two parts: the system of approach, then the system on the roundabout.

First, the approach. You are in the left-hand lane, and since you will be going all the way round the roundabout to reach your exit you need to change position to the right-hand lane. This has the practical advantage of allowing traffic going left or straight across to be on your left side, so they do not subsequently have to cut across your path.

1 Look behind.
2 Signal that you are going to move right. Use your indicators to signal and leave them on until you are in position on the roundabout.
3 Adjust your speed and change to a lower gear.
4 Give a lifesaver.
5 Move smartly into the right-hand lane.

You are now on course, and nearing the roundabout. Your indicator lights are continuing to signal a right turn. As before, give way to any traffic on the roundabout, but otherwise keep going. Give a lifesaver to the left just as you enter the roundabout.

Once on the roundabout:

1 Go straight across to the centre island and hold your position close to the island.
2 Carry on round until you have cleared the exit just before your intended exit.
3 Switch your indicators to signal left, look left, and manoeuvre left so that you are in position on the roundabout's outer rim.
4 Just before exiting, give a lifesaver left to be sure another vehicle (a faster motorbike, perhaps) isn't trying to overtake you on that side.

Of course, not every roundabout is laid out like the usual textbook example of four entrance/exit roads at 90-degree angles. Many have five or more roads leading off at various angles. But the system still applies; treat the first exit as a left turn, the second exit as straight across, and the third or subsequent exits as a right turn. The system applies on a mini-roundabout as well, but you may have to adjust it according to the amount of space you have. Taking a short cut across the centre of a mini-roundabout is to be discouraged.

1 On the approach, take up position just to the left of the centre line.

2 Slow down in the right-hand entry lane, be prepared to give way, and give a lifesaver left before moving onto the roundabout.

3 On the roundabout, move over towards the centre island.

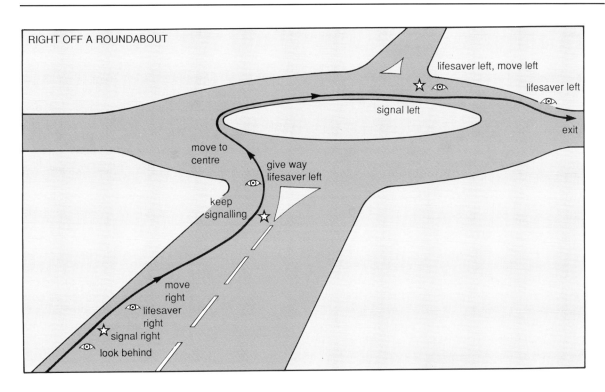

RIGHT OFF A ROUNDABOUT

lifesaver left, move left

lifesaver left

signal left

exit

move to centre

give way
lifesaver left

keep signalling

move right

lifesaver right

signal right

look behind

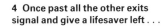

4 Once past all the other exits signal and give a lifesaver left . . .

5 Move over to the left of the roundabout, ready to exit . . .

6 Give another lifesaver left, and exit.

Make no mistake about it, this is the most dangerous manoeuvre you will make on the road. Overtaking safely depends on your fast and accurate judgement about quickly-changing traffic conditions: oncoming traffic, the vehicle you intend to overtake, the vehicle behind you, vehicles in front of the one you want to overtake and the amount of clear road you can see ahead. The odds in favour of misjudgment are, unfortunately, rather high, and the consequences of misjudgment could be fatal.

First, you have to weigh up the amount of clear road you can see ahead, in relation to the speed of the vehicle you are overtaking and the speed you will be able to attain in order to complete the manoeuvre. If there is an oncoming vehicle ahead, you will also have to assess its speed. This can sometimes be very difficult to do. In addition, you need to look for any obstruction in the opposite lane ahead that would cause an oncoming vehicle to swerve into your path.

Second, you have to try to anticipate any deviation on the part of the vehicle you want to overtake. Is there any reason for the driver to accelerate, move out to the right or suddenly turn right? Look ahead for any obstruction on the left or side turning on the right that might give a clue as to his intentions. Obviously, you would respond to his signals, but very often signals come too late.

Third, what about the vehicle behind you? If he is showing signs of impatience – staying close on your tail and well out to the right – he is very likely to try to overtake you the moment you think it is safe to move out. It has to be said that if you are on a small bike (or in a small car) showing L-plates, some drivers will press you very hard.

Fourth, what about the vehicles in front of the one you want to overtake? If you find yourself in a queue, you must try to anticipate their movements as well. Do you have enough room to get back in after you have overtaken? What if one pulls out in front of you as you are overtaking? You can find yourself in a nasty spot with no escape route if he is going much slower than you – maybe even slowing for a right turn – and you can't get back in the queue.

A motorcycle is the ideal vehicle for overtaking. The power-to-weight ratio, even of a smaller machine, gives it good acceleration. It is easily manoeuvrable, and it takes up little space. Nevertheless, you must weigh up very carefully all the above factors before you commit yourself, and *if in doubt – don't*. Also, consider whether the overtaking manoeuvre is necessary. One of the saddest stories I know is of a motorcyclist who lost his life when overtaking where he shouldn't have. He was only a few hundred metres from a dual carriageway, where he could have overtaken safely and easily.

➤ You must assess the speed of oncoming traffic.

➤ Don't pass too close, and don't dither about.

➤ Make sure you can get back in with time to spare.

The system for overtaking is applied as follows:

1 Make sure the road ahead is clear of oncoming traffic as well as any other hazards – a crossroad, bend, pedestrian crossing, or any kind of obstruction on *either* side of the road.
2 Look behind to be sure the road behind is clear. You can't rely on mirrors because an overtaking car or bike might be in your blind spot.
3 Signal.
4 Change gear to improve your acceleration.
5 Lifesaver.
6 Move out, overtaking quickly and giving all possible clearance.
7 When you are well clear of the overtaken vehicle, give a lifesaver and then return to course.

Time your overtaking manoeuvre so you are never in a row of three vehicles abreast – the overtaken vehicle, you, and an oncoming vehicle. Very often there will appear to be plenty of room to get through three abreast. But if either of the other two deviates a little you will be in an awkward spot, with no escape route. Be sure you can complete the overtake before the oncoming traffic gets to you. If you are not sure, hold back until it clears.

A common fault is following too closely behind the vehicle you are waiting to overtake. If you drop back, you will give yourself far better visibility. Use the width of the road to position yourself where you can see down the road to the left as well as to the right. You can often get a better view ahead down the left side, especially if the road is bending that way. A sure sign of a bad driver, and a certain cause of irritation to others, is one who is content to tuck in close behind a slow-moving vehicle, making it all the more difficult for others to get past.

Passing parked cars

This is much less dangerous than overtaking moving vehicles, yet motorcyclists often get into trouble on this comparatively simple manoeuvre. The problem is not the parked vehicles themselves, but what may come out of them or from in between them. Inexperienced motorcyclists make the mistake of riding too close in to the left. The closer to the left you are, the more difficult it is for you to see what may emerge

◄ You never know what will appear from behind a parked car, so stay alert as you pass.

and the more difficult it is for you to be seen. If you are riding down a street lined with parked cars, stay as far out to the right as possible. Picture in your mind an open car door, and leave at least that much clearance. Doors open and people get out. Children, dogs, and balls come flying out. Give them room.

Keep looking ahead for clues. A puff of exhaust smoke suggest that someone is about to pull out. A person sitting inside a car is very likely to open a door and get out. A rolling ball may be followed by a child.

◄ Allow plenty of room as you ride past a car. Someone may open a door and get out!

You need to be especially careful when pedestrians are about. The number of pedestrians injured by motorcycles is out of proportion to the number of motorcycles on the road. It doesn't follow from this that motorcyclists are more reckless or irresponsible; the accident is as likely to be caused by an error or misjudgement on the part of the pedestrian. But irrespective of who is at fault, you still have a responsibility to care for the more vulnerable road user. Remember, pedestrians are less likely to see you and your bike than they are to see a bus or other motor vehicle. They often find it difficult to judge the speed of a motorcycle. They may be surprised to find you in places where they don't expect a motor vehicle to be – filtering between traffic queues, for example.

Take special care when approaching a zebra crossing (that is, one not controlled by lights). In theory, you don't have to stop until the pedestrian actually steps onto the crossing, but this is no time to split hairs. Watch for anyone waiting to cross. Slow down, and be prepared to stop. Consider giving the slowing-down arm signal as illustrated in the Highway Code. Don't be moved by courtesy to wave a pedestrian across; another vehicle may be bearing down on you with no intention of stopping. Never overtake on the approach to a zebra crossing. If cars are stopped at the crossing you may filter up to the head of the queue, but don't overtake a moving vehicle near the crossing, and bear in mind that other vehicles will not only block your view, but they will also block anyone else's view of you.

Pelican crossings are controlled by lights, and you must stop if red is showing (even if the crossing is empty). Unlike normal traffic lights, red at a Pelican crossing is followed by flashing amber and if there is no one actually on the crossing you may go ahead. But be especially wary here. At the same time you see flashing amber, people waiting on the pavement will see flashing green, and they may interpret this as a signal to cross.

☛ If you are stopping at a zebra crossing, give the slowing-down signal. Otherwise the driver behind may assume you are carrying on down the road, and smash into you.

☛ Be very careful when the amber light is flashing at a light-controlled crossing. Pedestrians see a flashing green light, and may think it is safe to cross.

Part three:
Passing your test

The driving test is designed to see if you can ride your bike safely, and to check whether you know and understand the Highway Code. The test will include riding on the road followed by an examiner who will give you instructions by radio. You will also be asked questions on the Highway Code; some of these questions will be about road signs and markings, so it might be helpful to start this section by reviewing them.

Signs and markings are not placed on the road just to tell you what to do. They are there to help you read the road, to anticipate changes in road conditions, and to plan ahead. There is a system to traffic signs, based on shape and colour, and if you understand the system you will be better able to use the signs to your riding advantage.

Round signs give an order (think of the round 'O' in 'order'). A round sign that is predominantly blue gives a positive order – that is, something you *must* do. For example, a round blue sign with a white arrow is pointing in the direction you must go. A round sign on red gives a negative order – something you must *not* do. For example, a motorcycle circled in red means no motorcycling.

There are two very important signs that give an order but are not round. One is the 'Stop' sign. This is an internationally recognised traffic sign which is octagonal in shape. The other is the 'Give Way' sign which is triangular, with the triangle pointing down.

All other triangular signs give a warning. (You will note that the triangle is pointing up on these warning signs.) Warning signs indicate problems or hazards on the road ahead. They give you time to adjust your speed and gear down if necessary. Don't ignore them, and don't wait until you are on top of the hazard to respond to it. By then, it may be too late.

☞ **Round signs give orders – in this case, no motorcycles!**

Other signs give information and directions, and are mainly rectangular or square. They are also colour coded: blue signs are for motorways and direct you to a motorway; green signs give directions and distances on major roads, and white signs refer to local roads.

The markings along the centre of the road are especially helpful when it comes to reading the road. The centre line of a road is normally marked by short, broken white lines. When these lines start to tighten up, and become long white markings with short gaps, you know that the road is about to change in some way. It may be narrowing or you may be approaching a bend, crossroad or roundabout. In effect, it is a hazard warning line, and it gives you time to prepare for the hazard. It is permissible to cross over a hazard warning line if you can see the way ahead is clear.

If you have a solid white line on your side of the centre line you must not cross over it. (The Highway Code gives three exceptions to this rule. Find out what they are.) This is not the same as saying that you must not overtake where the line is solid. If you can safely overtake without going over the line you may do so. But bear in mind that the line is there because of a particular hazard so proceed with great care.

♦ **When the dotted white lines down the centre of the road begin to close up, it indicates a hazard. Be aware of the road markings – they are there to help you.**

These are some of the questions you might be asked on your test. Know the answers. We aren't going to make it easy for you by giving you the answers in this book. You will have to look them up in the Highway Code. But to give you some guidance, we have shown the paragraph or page where you will find the answer.

1 What are the legal requirements for your tyres? (Page 67)
2 What does the Highway Code say specifically about motorcyclists and moped riders? (Pages 70–71) And about pillion passengers? (Page 71)
3 What does the Highway Code say about excessive fumes, smoke and noise? (Page 69)
4 What must you do if you are involved in an accident? (Page 70)
5 What are the national speed limits for cars and motorcycles? (Page 48)
6 What is the shortest overall stopping distance at 30mph? What is it at 70mph? (Page 14)
7 When are you permitted to cross double white lines in the centre of the road when the line nearer to you is solid? (Para 71)
8 What is the meaning of white diagonal stripes or white chevrons painted on the road? (Para 73)
9 When may you overtake on the left? (Para 88)
10 What is a box junction? What should you do if you come across one? (Para 99)
11 What is the meaning of flashing headlamps? (Para 122)
12 When should you not use your horn? (Para 123)
13 When are you allowed to park your motorcycle on the road at night without leaving the lights on? (Para 131)
14 What does the Highway Code say about driving onto a level crossing? (Para 186)
15 What arm signal does the Highway Code recommend on the approach to a zebra crossing? (Page 52)

16 What are the special things you must do, and not do, when riding in fog? (Para 55)
17 How should you join a motorway? (Para 158-159)
18 What should you do if something falls off your bike while riding on a motorway? (Para 174)
19 Which lane should you use on a motorway? (Para 164-165)
20 What is the meaning of the coloured studs on motorways? (Para 166)
21 When are you allowed to stop on a motorway? (Para 180) Where may you park? (Para 181)
22 What should you be especially careful about when you leave the motorway? (Para 185)

A failure on the part of a person to observe a provision of the Highway Code shall not of itself render that person liable to criminal proceedings of any kind, but any such failure may in any proceedings (whether civil or criminal . . .) be relied upon by any party to the proceedings as tending to establish or to negative any liability which is in question in those proceedings.

This little paragraph is hidden away on the Contents page of the Highway Code, but it is one of the most significant statements in the Code. What it says, once you penetrate the legal language, is that you may not necessarily be breaking the law when you fail to observe something in the Highway Code. But if you are involved in an accident, your failure could be used against you in a criminal or civil trial. For example, the Highway Code recommends (Para 28) that motorcyclists should wear something light-coloured or bright. This is not a legal requirement, but if you get knocked off your bike while wearing all black leathers – even if the other driver is totally at fault – and the case comes to court, the defence will plead that you contributed to the negligence. Your damages could possibly be reduced accordingly.

In 1989 the Department of Transport introduced a new kind of motorcycle test. The examiner now follows the candidate on another motorcycle (or occasionally in a car) giving directions by one-way radio. This allows the test to cover more ground and a greater variety of road conditions. While it is doubtless a more demanding test, it is also fairer and more realistic than the old-style test where the examiner followed you on foot.

When you arrive at the test centre, park your bike and follow the signs directing you to a waiting room. Stay there until the examiner arrives. You shouldn't have long to wait, and it's a good idea to stay in your riding gear to save time. The examiner will want to see your driving licence and DL 196, and will ask you to sign a form. He will then compare the signature on your licence with your signature on the form. Next, he will fit you up with the radio equipment. This will consist of an earphone that fits inside your helmet, and a radio receiver strapped around your waist. The radio is voice-activated, and the examiner will ask if he may use your first name before each instruction to activate the microphone.

Outside, he will ask you to read a number plate as a simple eyesight test. He will check out the radio equipment with you to make sure everything is in order, and off you go.

The general instruction will be to carry on straight ahead, unless road signs or directions from the examiner indicate otherwise. The examiner will give you simple and concise directions like, 'turn right at the next junction'. If you fail to understand a direction, or if you get separated by traffic, you should stop and wait. You will be given directions in good time, so don't hesitate at every road junction waiting to hear something. Just keep riding normally.

After a short 'settling-down' ride, the examiner will stop you for the emergency stop. He will ask you to ride a left-hand circuit around the block, and stop when he signals you to do so. There won't be any element of surprise in the test, and as long as you use both brakes and stop under control you shouldn't find it difficult. Don't signal or give rear observation before you brake – remember this is supposed to be an emergency stop.

Next, the examiner will ask you to do a U-turn in the road. You can stop at the side of the road if you wish before starting the turn. The important thing to remember is that you *must* use rear observation before starting the manoeuvre. Signals are not necessary. Touching a foot down once or twice as you make the turn would not incur a penalty, but you must *ride* around, not paddle with your feet. At some point you will also have to do a hill start, to show that you can move off smoothly on a gradient. Another test will be an 'angle' start. This involves stopping behind an obstruction at the side of the road – a parked car, perhaps – and moving off at an angle.

Thereafter you will ride through a variety of town traffic and the open road. You will be expected to demonstrate that you understand road markings and traffic signs, that you know the correct procedure at roundabouts, junctions and pedestrian crossings, and that you can plan ahead for bends, changing speed limits, and other changing road conditions. Try to ride normally. If you're on a 30mph road, and traffic and road conditions are good, ride close to 30mph – don't ride timidly at 15. If you are on an open, 60mph road and conditions are good, keep up your speed. 'Failure to make adequate progress' is a frequent cause of test failure.

Do not use arm signals unless there is a special reason for doing so. The only arm signal the examiner will expect to see (if there is need for it) is the slowing-down signal at the approach to a pedestrian crossing.

At some point, the examiner may stop you for a slow riding exercise. You will simply have to ride in a straight line at walking pace for about 25 metres. When you complete the road test and return to the centre, the examiner will ask you a few questions about the Highway Code and other motoring matters. He will show you a number of road signs and markings on cards, and you will have to explain exactly what they mean.

At last the moment has come when he will tell you whether you have passed the test. If you have taken advantage of good training and put what you have learned into practice, and if you have remembered the things we have told you in this book, you should pass with no problem.

Part four:
After the test

You've passed the test. Congratulations! You've now opened up all kinds of new motorcycling possibilities. You can ride a larger, more powerful bike. You can take a friend on the back. You can use the motorways if you wish (though a lot of motorcyclists find motorways pretty boring, and use other roads when they can). You can take your bike abroad, something you couldn't do with a provisional licence.

But passing the test only means that you have satisfied a bureaucratic requirement for doing certain things in a prescribed way. It does not mean that you are a skilled motorcyclist. Real skill is something that will come only with time, experience, and perhaps further, more advanced training. Now that the test is behind you, you should start working at something I have mentioned before in this book; defensive riding.

Defensive riding is not something we can teach you. I can describe it here, and give lots of examples, but essentially it is a state of mind you adopt when riding which you have to develop yourself.

To start off, it might be easier to explain what it is not. To ride defensively is not to ride timidly. It is not always riding slowly, always riding cautiously along in the gutter, always fearful of using the power and speed at your disposal, always holding back, and always yielding to everything and everybody on the road. In fact, if you rode like that I would judge you to be an unsafe, incompetent motorcyclist. You can be a defensive rider, and still ride fast – within the constraints of speed limits and traffic conditions – positively, in control of your bike and in command of your roadspace.

There are three main elements to defensive riding: anticipation, planning and control.

Anticipation

Expect the unexpected. Most of the time traffic moves along in a well-ordered fashion. Vehicles seem to be maintaining more-or-less constant speeds and distances from one another. While a lot may be happening, it appears to be happening in an orderly, predictable way. Before long, you've put your mind in neutral and are just cruising along. Then, the unexpected occurs. Traffic ahead suddenly comes to an abrupt halt. A car pulls out in front of you. By the time you realise what's happened it may be too late.

The defensive rider is continuously scanning for signs and clues to help predict this kind of occurrence. There had to be a reason why the traffic ahead suddenly stopped. Was I looking for it? That car had to come from somewhere. Did I see that side street? Was I looking for something to emerge? As your mind begins to work in this fashion, the unexpected soon becomes the expected.

Planning

As you anticipate situations, you must plan to deal with them. To repeat what I have said several times before, you can't wait until you are on top of a problem to react to it. You need to plan your action ahead of time, which really comes down to placing yourself in the right position, in the right gear, at the right speed and with an available escape route if things go wrong. We don't have to look far to find good examples.

- Approaching a bend you need to judge how sharp it is. Even if you can't see all the way round the bend, you should be able to pick up clues – road signs or markings, actions of other vehicles, the angle of the verge, the line of the hedge or row of buildings. Having assessed the bend, you can plan your approach to it, choose your position, and select your speed and gear.
- You are approaching a junction. How much of the side road can you see? Plan your approach so that you are where other drivers can see you and you can see them. Drop down a gear so the power is there if you need it. Watch that car sitting poised on the left; have an escape route ready if the driver decides to pull out.
- You're a London commuter stuck in an early morning traffic jam. A timid rider might be content to sit in the jam. A skilful rider will take advantage of his machine's narrow profile to filter through the queues. A skilful *and* defensive rider will plan his moves very carefully: he will take care not to get caught with no escape, he will always have a hole to tuck into (a gap in the queue, or a space beside a small car or another bike), and he will not let himself be trapped between two vehicles or between a vehicle and the kerb.

Control

Keep control in your hands. Don't rely on the actions of anyone else. Never let your safety depend on the other road user acting reasonably and properly. Control is best explained through a few examples:

- You see a pedestrian standing on the kerb ahead, obviously waiting for a chance to dash across the road. Is he going to stay put until you are clear? You move as far out to the right as you can to give yourself more manoeuvring room and better visibility. You sound a short horn note.

♦ **Just because you have right of way, don't assume that others will respect it. In this position, you should be prepared for the car to pull out in front of you.**

♦ **Anticipate the actions of others. The small van here was bound to pull out to pass the parked truck, so an attempt to overtake it could have been disastrous.**

- There is a long queue of oncoming traffic ahead, following a slow-moving tractor. You can see one car edging out to the centre of the road, clearly impatient to get past. Will he overtake in your path, expecting to get by? You move well over to give him room, and drop down a gear to give yourself needed power.
- You are being hard pressed by a car right behind you. Will he try to overtake even though there's a bend just ahead? If he does, he will have to cut back in very sharply. You make sure he's got room to get past you and back in again without cutting you up.

In each of these situations you were able to apply defensive riding: you anticipated another's foolish action; you planned how you would respond before it happened, you were thereby able to keep in control when it did happen. Situations will develop, of course, that no rider could anticipate or avoid. Moreover, as fallible human beings, the time will come when attention wanders and concentration fails. But the more we condition ourselves to ride defensively, the more we will stack the odds in our favour.

When you were a learner you were probably taught to ride well to the left. When you took your DSA test, the examiner was looking to see how well you observed the basic Highway Code injunction, 'keep to the left except when overtaking or turning right'. But that is not always the best advice for a motorcyclist. Once your test is behind you and you start working to reach a higher standard, the basic rule should be 'use the width of the road'. This is a major advantage motor-cyclists have over drivers on four wheels. They haven't much road width to use, relative to the width of their vehicles, but you have – and you should use it to your benefit. But you must use the lifesaver. You can't safely manoeuvre right and left on the road without being very certain of what's behind you.

We have already considered positioning with reference to parked cars, pedestrians and cross roads. The more you are out to the right, near the centre of the road, the better you can see and be seen. Positioning is also important in preparing to overtake. By dropping well back behind the vehicle ahead you get a wider view. Then you can use the width of the road to manoeuvre to where you can see both to the left and to the right.

Positioning is probably the most critical single factor in cornering, or riding around a bend. This is for two reasons. First, you get a far better view around the bend, depending on your position. Second, you can use the width of the road to 'straighten out the bend', that is, effectively to make it less sharp. Let's see how this works on both right-hand and left-hand bends.

You would usually approach a right-hand bend by riding well into the left. This will give you a better view ahead than if you were positioned near the centre. As soon as you have a clear view you should then follow a gradual curve toward the centre of the road. As you near the completion of the bend you then ease back to the normal position towards the left. By following the bend this way you have, in effect, made it a more gradual one.

You take the opposite approach on a left-hand bend. Come in towards the centre of the road, follow a curve towards the left verge and then back to the normal position. It might be helpful to imagine the bend of the road as part of a full circle – the sharper the bend the smaller the radius of the circle. Then imagine the line you take also as part of a full circle. Your objective should be to ride the line of a circle

→ **A position well to the left will give you a better view on a right-hand bend.**

→ **Keep as far out to the right as is safe on a left-hand bend, and you'll see the oncoming traffic sooner.**

which has a larger radius than the circle of the bend, thereby making the bend easier to negotiate. Have a look at the diagram, and you'll get the idea.

One final comment before we leave the subject of bends. I mentioned earlier that you should try to judge the sharpness of a bend before you're actually in it. This may be difficult if there are no signs, road marking or roadside features. One technique is to view the angle at which the two verges appear to meet. As you approach a bend, the left verge and the right verge will appear to merge, and form the point of an arrow. Now watch that point as you draw nearer. If it seems to remain fixed – that is, if visibility doesn't open up – then the bend is a sharp one. If the point melts away as you approach then the bend is an easier one.

◆ Once you can see the road is clear on a right-hand bend, move towards the centre of the road. This way, you will effectively increase the radius of the bend, making it easier to negotiate.

◆ You can judge the sharpness of a bend by assessing the angle made by the two verges.

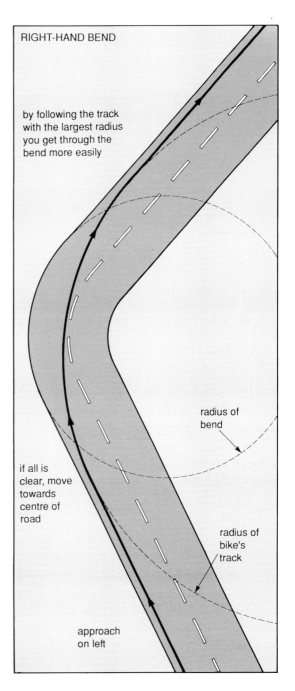

RIGHT-HAND BEND

by following the track with the largest radius you get through the bend more easily

radius of bend

if all is clear, move towards centre of road

radius of bike's track

approach on left

A sharp bend is something you will never find on a motorway. This is one reason why motorways are safer than other roads – in terms of vehicle miles travelled – and also why they are not much fun for motorcycling. I have to admit to an intense dislike of riding on motorways, although my opinion has no doubt been influenced by the many hours spent on highly-congested stretches of the M1 and M25. It's the abrupt change from 70mph to 10mph that can be terrifying for a motorcyclist. The sight of a long row of brake lights ahead, when everything around me is doing 70 plus, is not my idea of joyful riding.

It has to be said, however, that motorways normally provide a quick way of getting from A to B, and they do have better accident rates than other kinds of roads. When traffic is well spaced and moving steadily they are not unpleasant to ride. But there is a tendency for traffic to bunch up on motorways, partly because of congestion and also because of bad driving techniques. This, plus high speed, means that when something does go wrong it goes very wrong indeed. A minor problem at 30-40mph becomes disastrous at motorway speeds.

The Highway Code contains good advice on motorway driving, and there is no need to duplicate it here. Something that should be emphasised, however, is lane discipline. I mentioned traffic bunching as a typical motorway hazard. This usually develops because traffic is moving slowly in the centre lane. The basic rule for motorways is to drive in the left-hand lane except when overtaking. When traffic is heavy, this rule becomes something of a nonsense, because moving in and out of the left-hand lane is a greater risk than staying in the centre. As long as there are slower vehicles in the left-hand lane you should hold a steady course in the centre, but never let yourself become an obstruction in the centre lane. Remember that certain heavy vehicles are not allowed to use the right-hand lane, so one thoughtless driver – or motorcyclist – sticking doggedly to the centre can be the cause of serious traffic bunching.

Never venture onto a motorway without mirrors. The lifesaver – that quick glance over your shoulder before every manoeuvre – is indispensable on motorways, but you cannot risk frequent, long looks behind at motorway speeds. You must use mirrors to keep track of the traffic coming up behind you.

Don't focus your attention solely on the vehicle in front of you. Look ahead, and watch what's going on there as well. If you see brake lights coming on two or three cars ahead, you're in a better position to react than if you wait until the car immediately in front of you slams on the brakes. This applies to other roads, of course, not only to motorways.

Rule Number One of motorcycling – day or night – is that you should be able to stop within the distance that you can see. It follows therefore that, at night, you must be able to stop within the area illuminated by your headlights. Electrical equipment on motorcycles has been much improved in recent years, and most bikes are now fitted with quartz halogen or quartz iodide lamps, which give far greater light intensity than the old tungsten bulbs. You can fit accessory lights if you do a lot of night riding. But no matter how good your equipment, you can see less well at night than by day, and you must adjust your speed accordingly.

As a motorcyclist, you will have to cope with a number of handicaps at night. You are more likely to get cold, so your reflexes will be slower and you will find it harder to concentrate. You will find that headlight dazzle is worse through a helmet visor than through a car windscreen, especially if your visor is scratched or if it's raining. You will also find that your visor is more likely to mist up in the cool of the night. In all probability you will be more tired than you were earlier in the day. It is self-evident, therefore, that you must ride with greater care, dress warmly, and make sure your visor is clean and scratch-free. Headlight dazzle can make night riding quite unpleasant. Try not to look directly into the lights – focus instead on the left-hand verge. If you meet a driver who fails to dip headlights don't retaliate. Two blinded drivers hurtling towards each other are more dangerous than one.

Having said all of that, I would also say that some of my happiest riding memories are of warm summer nights, when there was just my bike and me, a star-lit sky and an empty road. At times like that you feel an affinity with your bike which is never there in the bustle of daytime traffic.

♦ **Motorways can be boring, but any lapse of concentration at motorway speeds could be disastrous, so be careful.**

♦ **Visibility is severely restricted at night, and the lights can generate a lot of glare. Keep a clear visor – and a clear head.**

To a motorcyclist, the road surface is much more immediate, real and tangible than it is to a car driver. It's right there. You can look down at it. No matter how fast you're going, you can reach down with your toe and touch it. Furthermore, your two wheels are far more sensitive than four wheels to the condition of the road surface. The driver of a four-wheel vehicle can often pass unknowingly over surface hazards that would have you sitting in the gutter. You must develop a very keen awareness of road surface conditions, and know how to look for clues to changes.

In the section on braking we discussed how a wet road surface affects your braking efficiency. Tyres simply do not have as firm a grip in the wet as they do in the dry, and this affects other movements as well as braking. Everything that you do – braking, accelerating, cornering – must be taken at a gentler pace in the wet, without sudden movement. This means planning ahead and lower speeds.

Surface problems

We tend to think of surface problems as related to bad weather such as rain and snow. But problems also arise in warm dry weather. Fresh grass cuttings on the road, or an accumulation of fallen leaves can become a slippery mass, so take care if you see the mowing machine at work or if you're out on an autumn day. You can easily skid on loose gravel and chippings – not to mention what they do to your paintwork. Take heed of the signs warning of this hazard. Remember, loose gravel often accumulates near the verge when the rest of the road is clear, so choose your line accordingly. In the summer of 1989 a few motorcyclists learned that melting tarmac makes a hazardous surface as well. It's not something that happens very often in Britain, but watch for it in extreme heat.

Spilt diesel fuel is a hazard in any weather. You will find it at the worst places – roundabouts, 'Give Way' junctions – where you are likely to be braking or cornering, and it's difficult to see in time. Some riders develop a nose for it. Spilt diesel is less of a problem now than it was a few years ago, thanks to efforts of groups like the British Motorcyclists Federation which campaigned for more secure fuel caps on buses and heavy vehicles.

Look out for overbanding. This is a smooth, dark-coloured, bituminous substance used to seal surface joins and road repairs. It becomes very slippery when wet, and is known to have been the causes of many motorcycle accidents. The Department of Transport has issued guidelines to road contractors on the use of overbanding. It should not, for example, be wider than about 5cm (2 in). I have seen it 30cm (12 in) or more wide in many places. If you find overbanding is a problem in your area, take it up with your local authority.

Another problem created by road contractors is cold-planing. This is when the road is scraped into transverse or diagonal grooves, in preparation for resurfacing. Coming upon it on two wheels is a weird sensation. It is probably less dangerous than it feels, but it can be unsettling to the inexperienced rider. Again, watch for the road-works warning sign, and respond accordingly.

As far as possible, try to avoid anything on the road that could affect the grip of your tyres – manhole covers, metal studs, white-painted arrows and lines – all the things that councils and road builders delight in scattering about. Most of the time you will pass right over them without incident. But there are times when a tyre is at the limit of its adhesion – either because of the condition of the tyre, the road, or something the rider is doing. At such times even a

◆ Try to steer clear of overbanding. It can be very treacherous in wet weather.

small metal stud is enough to cause the tyre to lose grip and topple you over. You can't be zig-zagging all over the road to avoid every object on it, but where possible choose a line that will take you clear of the more prominent hazards.

Ice

The worst hazard you will have to deal with is black ice. You can't see it and you won't know it's there until you and your motorbike have parted company painfully. Your only defence is to know when and where to expect it. Black ice occurs on bright, crisp winter mornings. It is almost always a morning phenomenon, rarely forming in the evening. The air temperatures can be as high as +5°C, but the sky will usually be clear. You are unlikely to encounter black ice on overcast mornings, and certainly not in the rain. (Freezing rain is something else, and thankfully very rare.) You will find black ice on open stretches of road, unprotected by overhanging trees or tall buildings. For this reason, it is mainly a country hazard, less often found in towns. The only way you can protect yourself is to stay in bed an hour longer, giving the warming daylight time to clear this menace from the road.

In general, freezing conditions and two wheels do not mix. There are no special techniques for riding in these conditions, other than the precautions we

Snow can be bad news on a bike. Use your common sense, and take the bus if it starts to snow in earnest.

have already mentioned. Keep to the main roads, which are more likely to be clear, and stay out of the gutter, where slush and ice may accumulate. When conditions really deteriorate, the best advice is leave your bike at home and take the bus. Fortunately, British winters are such that motorcyclists can ride all but perhaps a few days of the year, unlike some other European countries and American states where bikes are laid up for three or four months. Riding on a wet winter's day is not much fun, but it can be safe enough if you ride sensibly.

Fog

This is one weather hazard that is a special menace for motorcyclists. It can occur at any time of the year, and sometimes come on quite unexpectedly. You will find it almost impossible to keep your visor or goggles clear of fog, and you may have to remove your eye protection altogether. Since this will force you to slow down, it may be no bad thing. You will become even more difficult for others to see; bikes have fewer lights than cars, and not many are fitted with high-intensity rear lights.

The first thing you must do is *slow down*. It seems obvious, and yet every year we read about pile-ups in fog caused by speeding. When fog is really thick your best course is to ride near the verge or kerb. This way you know where you are and can see the road features. You also have a chance of escape if things start piling up around you. If another driver is pressing on you from behind, don't be intimidated into speeding up. Pull right over so he's forced to go around.

One trick in fog is to tag onto the tail lights ahead. This is helpful up to a point, but you must be especially careful to keep a safe distance – the vehicle may come to a dead stop if it hits something, and you won't even see brake lights. Don't allow yourself to become mesmerised by the lights of the vehicle ahead. If the driver suddenly turns off you will have no sense of where you are. It would be most unwise to try to overtake. You may not see the lights of oncoming traffic – some drivers still use sidelights only in fog – and if you do see lights you may totally misjudge speed or distance.

Whether you use your bike for commuting or for a camping holiday, you will want to be able to carry things on it. You can in fact carry quite a lot on a bike with a little planning and ingenuity, but you need to know something about weight distribution and correct loading. The ideal place to carry weight is near the apex of a triangle the base of which is a line between the front and rear wheel axles. The further away from the apex you place the weight, the more it can adversely affect the machine's handling.

Many motorcycles, including most smaller ones, have a luggage rack fitted behind the pillion seat. Riders secure objects to the rack or attach a topbox on it. This is a convenient place to carry gear, and topboxes have the advantage of being lockable and fairly secure, but bear in mind that the weight is now well outside the area of the triangle – in fact it is behind the rear axle. A moderate amount of weight back there is acceptable, but if you overload the rear end you will lighten the front and seriously impair steering.

A lot of touring bikes have panniers fitted on both sides, just over the rear wheel. Weight distribution is good, since the load is carried immediately over the rear axle. The panniers can be locked and they are reasonably secure. They are favoured by long-distance travellers because they are usually of the quickly-detachable kind which can be taken off and carried like small suitcases. Some riders like to use saddlebags, which don't require any permanent

☛ **Saddlebags are a useful alternative to panniers.**

attachments to the bike. You simply throw the bags over the seat and sit on them. You have to take them with you when you leave the bike, of course, since there is no way to secure them. There is also the possibility that they will chafe the side panels or possibly come into contact with the hot exhaust pipe.

Another favourite is the tank bag, which straps on over the petrol tank just in front of the rider. This is probably the ideal in terms of weight distribution, and you can also display a map, directions, address or whatever inside a plastic cover. But capacity is limited, they can be a bother when filling the tank, and there is a danger of scratching your paintwork.

☛ **Panniers provide a surprising amount of luggage space. These are permanently fixed to the bike, but will easily accommodate a large holdall apiece.**

☛ **For moderate loads, try a backpack. You can carry quite a lot on your shoulders without strain, and when you leave the bike, you take your gear with you.**

Many of the racing-style bikes popular today, and some trail bikes, don't have any means of carrying luggage. In this case, your best bet is probably a backpack carried on your own shoulders. Within reason, you can carry a fair amount without feeling the burden, and since it's with you at all times you don't have to worry about your gear being stolen.

Anything you attach to your bike – a topbox, panniers or a fairing for weather protection – can affect handling and steering. Use some common sense, and don't fit a small machine with a massive accessory. It can spoil the looks as well as the handling of your bike. Fairings especially can impair steering unless they are designed for your bike and properly fitted.

Get some competent advice before you lash out a lot of money on something that could ruin your motorcycle.

Taking a passenger

Now that you have passed your test you will be able to take a friend on the back. Two-up motorcycling is a lot of fun, and unless you have two large people on one small bike, machine handling will not be much affected. In fact, on a larger machine you will scarcely be aware the passenger is there, provided he or she follows a few simple rules:

- Sit still.
- Keep your feet on the footrests even when the bike is stopped, unless you're getting off.
- Leave signalling to the driver.
- Above all, *don't lean opposite to the lean of the bike*. That's a sure way to ruin a beautiful friendship.
- Relax and enjoy the ride.

The law requires pillion passengers to wear a helmet. There are specific references to passengers in the Highway Code (page 71) which you should read carefully.

To the 'driver', one sober word. Bear in mind that the life of your passenger is totally in your hands. He or she is completely at the mercy of your riding. Unlike the passenger in a car, there is nothing a person on the pillion seat can do to take control of the bike or avert an accident. This is no time for you to be stupid or show off.

Many motorcyclists like to do all their own maintenance. They enjoy it and believe that if you want a job well done you should do it yourself. It is possible that you won't have the time, the tools, the skill or the interest to do it all yourself, but there are a few basic jobs that you should be able to do. Even if you let your dealer do all the servicing, you will want to know that the job was done properly. Read the handbook that comes with your bike. The information that handbooks give you nowadays tends to be pretty superficial, but it will be enough for most basic checks. If you buy secondhand, try to get the handbook (and the tool kit) from the seller. If he doesn't have it you may be able to buy one from a dealer. You can also get a workshop manual for your particular bike if you want to get deeper into maintenance.

Brakes

Your bike will be fitted with disc or drum brakes. Most smaller bikes have drum brakes front and rear, but many are now fitted with discs in front. In fact, drum brakes are probably better on small bikes, and discs are not really necessary on anything under about 250cc. But manufacturers put them on to promote that 'big bike' image.

If you have a disc brake, it won't require much maintenance. You have to be sure the brake fluid is topped up, but since the fluid reservoir is usually mounted prominently on the handlebar it doesn't require much effort to check the level. Occasionally you should look at the disc pads to make sure they haven't worn excessively. Your handbook should tell you how to check for wear. Don't wait until the pads start scoring grooves on the disc itself; once they do this it becomes fairly expensive to repair.

A drum brake on the front wheel is operated by a cable running from the brake lever on the handlebar to the front wheel axle. Cables stretch with use, and you need to make an adjustment from time to time.

Apply the front brake lever firmly. It should come back so that it is parallel to the handlebar, about 3cm from it. If you can draw it right back to the handlebar then you need to make an adjustment.

There will be an adjustment nut either next to the brake lever or down near the axle. Sometimes you

If you can squeeze the lever close to the handlebar like this (above), then the front brake needs adjusting. Tighten the nut by the lever (below) to take up the tension.

will find one in both places. All you have to do is tighten the nut to take up the tension on the cable. When you have finished, spin the front wheel to make sure you haven't overdone it. If the wheel binds, let off the tension a bit.

Inside the brake drum are two 'shoes' which press against the drum when you apply the brake, and slow the wheel rotation. The shoes wear with use, and eventually need replacing. On most bikes you will find a wear guide – usually a pair of arrows that line up when you apply the brake – so you can easily see when the shoes are due for replacement.

A drop of oil at either end of the brake cable will keep it working smoothly. (We once had a learner who oiled his brakes to stop them squeaking, but of course you wouldn't do anything that stupid.) If you see any signs of fraying or wear on the cable, have it

If you have more than 4–5 cm of free play on the brake pedal (above), it is time to adjust the rear brake. Tighten the nut on the link rod (below).

You may have to reset the brake light switch (above) after adjusting the rear brake. A wear guide on the brake drum (below) will show you when the brake shoes are worn.

replaced. The last thing you want is for a cable to snap when you need your brakes.

The same principle applies on a rear drum brake, except in this case the brake is activated by a link rod running from the brake pedal to the rear axle. You should have about 4–5cm of free play on the pedal; more than that and it's time for an adjustment. You make this adjustment by turning a nut on the link rod.

In addition to checking wheel spin, you also need to check the brake light when you have finished. An adjustment of the brake can alter the brake light setting so that it doesn't come on at all when you apply the rear brake, or else it stays on continuously. A simple turn of the screw on the brake light switch (you will find it near the brake pedal) is all you need to put it right.

← Spin the rear wheel after adjusting the brake to make sure that you haven't over-tightened it. Do the same with the front wheel.

Tyres

The law has a lot to say about your tyres. So it should. Your tyres are your only contact with the road surface. Tyre grip stops you when you brake; tyre grip keeps you from falling over when you corner. Excessive wear, the wrong air pressure, or improper fitting *are serious safety hazards*. The Highway Code has the following to say about your tyres. Know it by heart, and apply it:

Make sure that your tyres are suitable for the vehicle, are properly inflated, have a continuous tread depth of at least 1mm across three quarters of the width, with visible tread across the remainder of the width, and are free from cuts and other defects.

➥ A 10p coin is a useful tread depth gauge: the rim of the coin is 1mm deep. Note the arrow on the tyre indicating the direction of rotation.

Let's look at these points in turn:

- 'Suitable for the vehicle'. There are different kinds of tyres for different kinds of bike. When you buy a replacement tyre, make sure it's one the tyre manufacturer recommends for your make and model. Most motorbike tyres are intended for either front or rear wheel fitting. Don't confuse them. Tyres are also speed-rated, and it would be foolish to fit a tyre with a low speed rating on a powerful motorcycle. Certain kinds of tyres are not legal for road use (racing tyres, off-road competition tyres). A reputable dealer will advise you if you're unsure.
- 'Properly inflated'. It is dangerous to ride on tyres that are either over- or under-inflated, and they will also wear out much faster. Spend a few pounds on your own air pressure gauge. That way, you can check pressures before you start off. (Tyres heat up as you ride causing a build-up of air pressure. You get a false reading unless you check pressure when the tyres are still cold.) Know what your tyre pressures should be – front and rear – and make sure you maintain that pressure. It may be necessary to increase the pressure when the bike is loaded or when you are carrying a passenger. Check your handbook.
- 'Tread depth of at least 1mm'. This is a *minimum* recommendation, and probably made with four-wheeled vehicles in mind. Tyres are important on cars, too, but not as critical as they are on bikes, and no experienced motorcyclist would ride on less than 2mm. Quite aside from the danger of a worn tyre, you can't carry a spare on a bike and a puncture is a major problem. Why risk it?
- 'Free from cuts and other defects'. This is self-evident. Check from time to time for sharp objects embedded in the tread which could cut into the tyre.

You also want to be sure your tyres are fitted correctly. Most tyres have a fitting line; when they are mounted on the wheel correctly, the fitting line should be parallel to the rim all the way round on both sides. There may also be an arrow embossed on the side of the tyre. The arrow should point in the direction of wheel rotation when the bike is moving forward. Make sure valve caps are in place. They will help to keep air in should there be a valve leak, but their main function is to prevent valve leaks by keeping dirt and grit out.

Lubrication

We touched on lubrication in the section on two-stroke and four-stroke engines. It is very important that you follow the manufacturer's instructions on this subject. If you don't, you will wear out your engine prematurely, and you might ruin it altogether.

If yours is a two-stroke machine, it's just a matter of keeping the oil reservoir topped up. Any good brand of two-stroke oil (but make sure it *is* two-stroke oil) from any of the major oil companies will do very nicely. If you have one of the older-style machines where you have to mix the oil in the petrol tank, then you should follow the manufacturer's instructions.

You also have to lubricate the gearbox on a two-stroke. This requires filling the gearbox reservoir with the recommended oil (not two-stroke), keeping it topped up, and changing it at regular intervals. Check the handbook for the recommended grade of oil, and the mileage intervals for changing it.

On a four-stroke machine, you have to make sure the oil level in the engine is topped up (there's usually a dip-stick or sight-glass so you can see) and you have to change it at recommended intervals. The handbook will tell you what grade of oil to use, and how often to change it. You don't have to worry about gearbox lubrication on a four-stroke.

Clutch

You will remember we described earlier how a clutch works: when you pull in on a handlebar lever, the clutch plates separate so you can change gear. The connection between the lever and the plates is a cable, and like the brake cable it will stretch with use, so you will need to adjust it occasionally. If the cable is too tight, the plates can't mesh together properly; if it's too loose they can't separate completely. (The former is known as 'clutch slip', the latter as 'clutch drag'.) Your handbook will tell you how much free play you should have on the cable – normally about 5mm. The nut for making the adjustment is usually found at the lever end.

A 2-stroke will need the oil in the engine reservoir topped up (above). You must also check the gearbox oil (below). Make sure you use the right oil for each.

You need this much free play on the clutch lever if it is to operate properly.

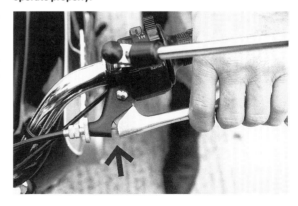

Chain

As you know, the chain transmits power from the gears to the rear wheel. It is a very efficient means of transmission, provided it is well-oiled and adjusted, but a slack, out-of-adjustment chain can waste 40 per cent or more of your engine power. (If you are on a moped or restricted 125, you do not have surplus power to throw away.)

To check and adjust the chain you need to get the rear wheel off the ground. This is easy enough if your bike has a centre stand. If not, you will need to get it up on a box or stand of some kind. Find the tightest point on the chain. (As you spin the rear wheel, the chain will rise and fall slightly. The high point of the rise is the tight point of the chain.) Check the tension at that point. You should have about 2–3cm of free play, but see what your handbook says.

If you need to adjust the tension, first loosen the rear axle nut. Your bike will have either a chain-adjusting nut or a snail cam on both sides of the rear wheel. The chain is tightened when you draw the rear wheel back by turning the nut or the cam on both sides. It is very important to make precisely the same adjustment on both sides. If you don't, you will pull the wheel out of alignment. When you have finished the job, tighten up all the nuts and check that the tension is right. Since you have moved the

rear wheel, you will also need to check that both the rear brake and brake light are still in proper adjustment.

Clean any grit and dirt off the chain with a lint-free cloth, then oil it. You can use one of the spray-on chain oils, or apply ordinary engine or gear oil with a squirt can. The best way to clean and lubricate a chain is to get a tub of specially-formulated chain grease. Remove the chain completely from the bike and coil it up in the tub of grease. Warm the grease on the kitchen stove (it makes an awful smell, so you won't be very popular) until it melts and thoroughly bathes the chain. When you replace the chain, make sure you get the spring link back on the way it came off – with the closed end facing the direction of the chain's rotation.

The chains on some large motorcycles have lubricants sealed in with small rubber O-rings. You shouldn't use solvents to clean these chains since they would damage the rings.

Chains wear and need replacement. To check, pull the chain back from the rear sprocket. If you can insert a pencil between the chain and the sprocket, it's a good sign that the chain is worn out. Sprockets wear, too. Check that the points are sharp and evenly pointed. If they're starting to look like the crest of an ocean wave, it's time to fit a new sprocket.

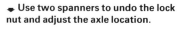

➤ Loosen the axle nuts (you may have to take out a split pin first).

➤ Use two spanners to undo the lock nut and adjust the axle location.

➤ Check that the axle is in the same position on each side.

Electrics

Make sure the battery is topped up with distilled water to the recommended level, and keep the terminals clean and free of corrosion. If your bike is going to be out of use for some time, it is a good idea to take the battery off and remove it to a place where you can charge it up from time to time. Know where the fuse box is, so you won't have to fumble around to find it on a dark and rainy night. (Fuses only blow on dark and rainy nights.) Make sure there is a spare fuse there if you need it. The same applies to bulbs. Carry a few spares, and know how to change them. It may be difficult to change a headlight bulb at the side of the road, but it is rare for both the high and low beam elements to go at the same time; if you have to ride home on high beam you can lower the aim of the headlight to avoid dazzling others.

Ignition

Look after your spark plugs. If a bike is hard to start the odds are the problem will be a faulty plug. Know how to take it out, clean it off, check the gap, and replace it. The main problem is a build-up of carbon particles on the gap. In order to get a spark, the electric current has to jump the gap. If it can simply flow across through a carbon particle you get no spark and your engine is lifeless. Most plugs require a gap of about 0.6–0.7mm (0.024–0.026in.) Use a feeler gauge to check and adjust the plug gap.

Steering

You don't want to get involved with the steering-head bearings on your motorcycle unless you really know what you are doing. But there is a simple test you should do from time to time to check for wear. The bearings are in the steering-head spindle where it meets the yoke of the handlebars. Ask someone to hold the rear of the bike so the weight is off the front wheel. Take a firm hold of the forks and shake them. Feel for any movement or sign of looseness in the steering-head spindle. Then allow the handlebars to turn from side to side. They should turn smoothly and freely. That's all there is to it. If there is a problem, ask your dealer to check it out or get some competent help if you need it.

◆ Check the steering at intervals – but don't try to do any adjustments yourself.

Exhaust system

There is not much you need to do with your exhaust. On two-strokes, you should take the baffle out every 5000 miles or so and clean it up. Otherwise it's mainly a matter of making sure the exhaust is in good repair and not punctured or rusted out. The public is intolerant of excessive motorcycle noise, and rightly so. There is no reason for it, and few things tarnish the image of motorcycling more. It is now illegal for dealers to sell exhaust systems that do not meet specified noise-suppression requirements, and it is illegal for you to use a silencer that is not working properly. There are some foolish people who think they can extract more power or speed from their bikes by tampering with the silencer. Don't believe it. It's far more likely to get you in trouble with the law, infuriate the neighbours, and damage your engine.

As we said in the beginning, motorcycling is a lot of fun and it can open up a new world of friends and activities for you.

Club life

Many motorcyclists are 'clubbable' people, and you might want to get started by getting involved in a club. There are clubs of all sizes and interests, ranging from the big national and one-make clubs, with branches and sections all over the country, to small, local groups. Your training scheme instructors might be club members, and will be glad to introduce you; some centres in fact are run by local clubs. A club can help you with spare parts, repairs or rebuilds and there are a lot of special interest groups for things like international touring, trail-riding, old bikes, sidecars. The BMF can put you in touch with a club, or maybe you and a group of like-minded friends would like to form your own.

But you don't have to be a club person. Many motorcyclists are staunch individualists who prefer riding on their own, or with one or two friends. There is nothing wrong with that; after all, a motorbike is very much a personal thing.

Foreign travel

My special interest is taking my bike abroad. Motorcyclists are very special kinds of travellers. They don't have to worry about airport delays, motorway congestion and package-tour crowds. They can get on their bikes and go when and where they want. Crossing over to the Continent is easily done, and except for the cost of the ferry ticket it is scarcely more expensive than a holiday at home. You don't even have to book the ferry in advance. Just show up at the dock; there's nearly always room for one more motorbike.

The legal requirements are not complicated. You need a passport of course, and you should get a 'green card' from your insurance company which extends your insurance cover to the countries you are visiting. As a tourist, your British driving licence is recognised in most European countries. However, Spain and Portugal require an International Driving Permit, and in Italy you need an Italian translation of your licence. You can get most kinds of documentation, travel insurance and maps from the RAC.

Modern motorcycles are reliable, and the only spares I bother to carry are a few light bulbs. If you do have

USEFUL ADDRESSES

Auto-Cycle Union (ACU)
Miller House, Corporation Street
RUGBY CV21 2DN

British Motorcyclists Federation (BMF)
129 Seaforth Avenue, Motspur Park
NEW MALDEN, Surrey KT3 6JU
Tel: 081 942 7914

BMF Rider Training Scheme
PO Box No 2
UCKFIELD, East Sussex TN22 3ND
Tel: 0825 712896

Institute of Advanced Motorists (IAM)
359 Chiswick High Road
LONDON W4 4HS

National Training Scheme (Star Rider)
Federation House
2309 Coventry Road
BIRMINGHAM B26 3PB

RAC Motoring Services
PO Box 700, Spectrum
Bond Street
BRISTOL BS99 1RB

mechanical problems or breakdown, you can get help as easily in other European countries as you can at home. It isn't necessary to have a large touring bike. You will get more enjoyment on the small country roads than on Continental motorways, and if you're in no great rush to get somewhere, a small bike will do you just as well. There are marvellous campsites on the Continent, ranging from the simple to the luxurious. If you are not a camper, or don't want to carry the gear, you can always find a modest bed-and-breakfast hotel. Again, there's no need to book ahead. In fact, the real joy of touring by motorbike is the total freedom it gives you to get on your bike and go, without a lot of tedious advance planning and preparation.

Trail-riding
A special kind of touring is trail-riding, or riding the green lanes, and there is ample opportunity for it in Britain. These are unsurfaced, unmade roads with vehicular rights of way, often following ancient, historic tracks. They are public roads, and all the legal requirements of licences, insurance and helmets apply. But riding the green lanes takes you far away from the bustle of today's traffic. As one trail-riding enthusiast described it, it's 'following in the footsteps of Roman legions, the tracks left by merchants and drovers, the relics of monastic trade routes, mail coaches . . . and invading armies.' The Trail Riders Fellowship is the national body of green lane riding, and the BMF can put you in touch.

Motorcycle sport
There is a wide range of motorcycle sport – road racing, motocross, trials, enduro, grass track. The governing body of motorcycle sport in Great Britain is the Auto-Cycle Union (ACU). If you think you might want to get involved as a competitor, marshall, scrutineer or time-keeper, get in touch with the ACU for information on how to start.

Advanced riding
If you have been riding for a while, have a full licence and maybe a larger bike, you may want to raise your riding skills to an even higher standard. There are a number of ways to learn and assess your advanced riding techniques. The Institute of Advanced Motorists will give you an independent evaluation of your riding skills by an expert motorcyclist. The BMF offers its Blue Riband Award, which comprises a high level of instruction based on Police Roadcraft, and an independent assessment.